⪢ ONE ⪡

A Mother's Sorrow

WHEN AMELIA CULVER met Paul Edmonson, she had no intention of ever marrying. Milly, as she was known, enjoyed spending time with Paul at church on Sundays, and the more she learned about him the more she cared for him, but she did not want to be his wife. She realized that she had fallen in love, but she was not concerned about love. Milly knew the truth: She was enslaved, and in Montgomery County, Maryland, in the early 19th century, her future did not belong to her.

At the time, Paul was enslaved on a nearby farm. They would not be able to live together as man and wife because they had different owners; but if they married, Milly and Paul would be able to see each other from time to time. Any children they might have would be born into bondage, owned by Milly's master. Milly understood that the joy of marriage and family would end in heartbreak when her children—her babies—grew old enough to be torn away from her to work or to be sold in the slave market.

Despite what seemed like inevitable sadness, Paul asked Milly to marry him. She turned him down. Milly longed for love and family, but still more, she longed for liberty. "I loved Paul very much," Milly said. "But I thought it wasn't right to bring children into the world to be slaves."

Milly's family and others at Asbury Methodist Church in Washington, D.C., urged her to reconsider Paul's offer, arguing that Paul was a good man and it was her Christian duty to marry and have children.

Paul proposed again, and this time she accepted.

UNITED STATES SLAVE TRADE.
1850.

The copper plate used to make this engraving was discovered by workmen clearing the ruins of Pennsylvania Hall in Philadelphia, which was built by the Pennsylvania Anti-Slavery Society. After it was completed, the building stood for only three days before it was burned to the ground by anti-black rioters on May 17, 1838.

"THIS CHILD ISN'T OURS"

As Milly had predicted, the painful realities of love within slavery soon followed. "Well, Paul and me, we was married, and we was happy enough," Milly said. "But when our first child was born I says to him, 'There 'tis now, Paul, our troubles is begun. This child isn't ours.

" 'Oh, Paul,' says I, 'what a thing it is to have children that isn't ours!'

Passenger on the Pearl

Also by Winifred Conkling

Radioactive!: How Irène Curie and Lise Meitner Revolutionized Science and Changed the World

Passenger on the Pearl

The True Story of Emily Edmonson's Flight from Slavery

WINIFRED CONKLING

ALGONQUIN YOUNG READERS
2016

Published by
ALGONQUIN YOUNG READERS
An imprint of Algonquin Books of Chapel Hill
Post Office Box 2225
Chapel Hill, North Carolina 27515-2225

a division of
WORKMAN PUBLISHING
225 Varick Street
New York, New York 10014

First paperback edition, Algonquin Young Readers, January 2016. Originally published
in hardcover by Algonquin Young Readers in January 2015.
Printed in the United States of America.
Published simultaneously in Canada by Thomas Allen & Son Limited.
Design: Anne Winslow and Steve Godwin. Layout: Jacky Woolsey.

PHOTO CREDITS
Getty Museum: Page 116; Library of Congress: Pages 2, 4, 5, 7, 12, 18, 21, 25, 27,
36–37, 40, 42, 48, 50, 64, 68, 69, 81, 82, 83, 86, 87, 89, 90, 101, 103, 111, 114, 121, 127,
128, 133, 138, 149; Louisiana State Museum: Page 67; National Archives: Page 58;
New York Public Library: Page 91; Onondaga Historical Society: Page 109;
Wikipedia Commons: 75, 108, 140.

Library of Congress Cataloging-in-Publication Data
Conkling, Winifred.
Passenger on the Pearl : the true story of Emily Edmonson's flight
from slavery / Winifred Conkling.—First edition.
pages cm
Includes bibliographical references.
ISBN 978-1-61620-196-8 (HC)
1. Edmonson, Emily, 1835–1895—Juvenile literature. 2. Pearl (Schooner)—
Juvenile literature. 3. Fugitive slaves—Washington Region—Biography—Juvenile
literature. 4. Fugitive slaves—Washington Region—History—19th century—Juvenile
literature. 5. Antislavery movements—Washington Region—History—19th century—
Juvenile literature. 6. Antislavery movements—United States—History—19th century—
Juvenile literature. 7. Underground Railroad—Washington Region—Juvenile literature.
8. Washington Region—History—19th century—Juvenile literature.
9. Edmondson family—Juvenile literature. I. Title.
E445.D6C66 2015
306.3'62092—dc23
[B]   2014029246

ISBN 978-1-61620-550-8 (PB)

10 9 8 7 6 5 4 3 2 1
First Paperback Edition

Contents

No man can tell the intense agony which is felt by the slave when wavering on the point of making his escape. All that he has is at stake; and even that which he has not is at stake also. The life which he has may be lost, and the liberty which he seeks, may not be gained.

FREDERICK DOUGLASS
My Bondage and My Freedom, 1855

"Paul, he says to me, 'Milly, my dear, if they be God's children, it ain't so much matter whether they be ours or no; they may be heirs of the kingdom.'" Milly tried to find peace in his words, but she still worried.

In the early years of her marriage, Milly and her young children lived with her mistress, Rebecca Culver, and Culver's married sister in Colesville, Maryland. It was not uncommon for an enslaved person to be freed when his owner died, and in 1821, Paul's owner freed him in her will. While many owners did not recognize slave marriages, Culver allowed Milly to work as a seamstress and live with Paul and their children on a local farm. Milly and Paul continued to have children, increasing Culver's wealth significantly.

"I had mostly sewing," Milly said. "Sometimes a shirt to make in a day—it was coarse like, you know—or a pair of sheets or some such, but whatever 'twas, I always got it done. Then I had all my housework and babies to take care of and many's the time after ten o'clock I've took my children's clothes and washed 'em all out and ironed 'em late in the night 'cause I couldn't never bear to see my children dirty. Always wanted to see 'em sweet and clean. I brought 'em up and taught 'em the very best ways I was able."

Culver was mentally challenged and she was never able to manage her finances on her own. In 1827, Culver's brother petitioned the court in Montgomery County to have her ruled legally incompetent. The judge agreed and named her brother-in-law, Francis Valdenar, as guardian of her business affairs, which included oversight of Milly and her children.

By the mid-1830s, Milly had given birth to fourteen children, eight girls and six boys. She lived in constant fear that they would be taken from her. "I never seen a white man come onto the place that I didn't think, There, now, he's coming to look at my children," Milly said. "And when I saw any white man going by, I've called in my children and hid 'em for fear he'd see 'em and want to buy 'em."

In time, Milly's fears were realized. As was common practice at the time, when any of her children reached age 12 or 13, he or she was taken from home and hired out to families in the Washington, D.C., area to live and work as domestic slaves. Their wages were sent back to Culver, who depended on this income.

Heartbroken, Milly begged her girls not to marry until they were free so that they would not become mothers of children born into slavery. She said, "Now, girls, don't you never come to the sorrows that I have. Don't you never marry till you get your liberty. Don't you marry to be mothers to children that ain't your own." Each of the Edmonson children, both the boys and the girls, shared their mother's belief that aside from their duty to God, nothing was more important than freedom.

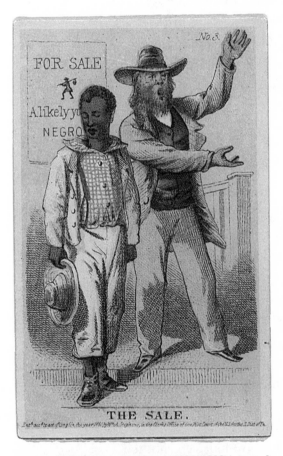

In 1863, Henry Louis Stephens (1824–1882) created this lithograph titled "The Sale." The image is the third in a 12-part series of antislavery trading cards titled "Journey of a Slave from the Plantation to the Battlefield." Abolitionists distributed the cards as a means of spreading their message.

AN UNCERTAIN FUTURE

Over the years, Valdenar had allowed the five oldest Edmonson sisters—Elizabeth, Martha, Eveline, Henrietta, and Eliza—to buy their freedom. They raised the money by taking on extra work and keeping a portion of their earnings, or by accepting money from family and friends. By 1848, Culver was in poor health, and she faced growing debts. Six of the Edmonson children were hired out at the time. There were no plans for their imminent sale, but the siblings realized that their futures were far from secure. Slave owners prized the Edmonson children for their honesty, intelligence, and morality; slave dealers prized them because they could demand a high price on the auction block. Would Valdenar sell one or more of them to pay Culver's expenses?

If they were sold, they could end up in fine homes working as domestics and butlers or they could end up in the Lower South, working as field hands or, worse yet, as "fancy girls" in the New Orleans sex trade. The two hired-out Edmonson sisters, Mary

PICKING COTTON ON A GEORGIA PLANTATION.

The Edmonson siblings feared being sold south to work in the fields as shown in this 1858 wood engraving of cotton picking on a Georgia plantation.

and Emily, had pale complexions and fine features, which meant that they could fetch a high price in the southern market. They were only 15 and 13 years old, respectively—a bit young to be sold into this line of work even by the standards of the time, but their true age did not matter. In such circumstances, slave traders were known to falsify documents and add a year or more to the reported age of their young female slaves.

All of the enslaved Edmonson children had discussed with their parents the possibility of running away. They faced difficult choices: If they stayed, they risked being sold south at their owner's convenience. If they ran away and were caught, they faced the likelihood that they would be sold to harsher owners in the South.

While she had not experienced such hardships herself, Emily had seen coffles of slaves shuffling down the streets of the city, men and women walking with shackles around their ankles and handcuffs on their wrists, paired together and linked by long metal chains. These human herds were driven like cattle or swine down Pennsylvania Avenue and the streets of Washington, D.C., chained together so that they could not flee while being moved from one place to another. Most coffles were bound for the Deep South to labor as field slaves on cotton and sugar plantations. Field slaves performed backbreaking work from sunrise to sunset, often under the watchful eye of an overseer with a bullwhip; house slaves spent their days cooking and cleaning and watching children.

The only option Emily and her enslaved brothers and sisters saw to ensure their freedom and safety was to flee—and to pray that they could avoid getting caught. When the Edmonson family learned of a bold escape planned for a spring night in April, they decided to take the chance. A lifetime of freedom was worth the risk of capture, they reasoned.

A woman outside a slave pen in Alexandria, Virginia. Her attire—a long skirt or dress made of an inexpensive, coarse fabric known as "slave cloth"—was typical of enslaved women in the mid-19th century.

≈ TWO ≈

Escape: April 15, 1848

EMILY EDMONSON WAITED in darkness. Some time near 9 p.m. she heard a handful of dirt scatter across her bedroom window. That was it: the signal.

She peeked outside and saw her older brother Samuel looking up from the shadows. She grabbed a small bag, snuffed out the candle by her bed, and tiptoed through the silent house. She slipped out the back door, leaving the house for the last time.

Emily walked along the dark streets, her brother by her side. She wore a plain, ankle-length dress with a wool shawl wrapped around her shoulders to protect against the chill. She had pulled her hair into a neat bun at the nape of her neck. Nothing about her appearance drew attention, but still her heart pounded, fast and steady.

When they were out of earshot, she asked Samuel, "What will Mother think?"

"Don't stop to think of her," Samuel said, not slowing his pace. "She would rather we'd be free than to spend time to talk about her."

Emily hurried to keep up. He was right. Of course he was right. Samuel was 21, a grown man, and she trusted him to keep her safe, as safe as possible. This was what Mother wanted; this was what they all wanted—to be free.

Emily and Samuel walked down Pennsylvania Avenue, past the north entrance to the Executive Mansion, the building later renamed the White House. Horse-drawn carriages passed them on the unpaved street, and they kept on, heads down to avoid

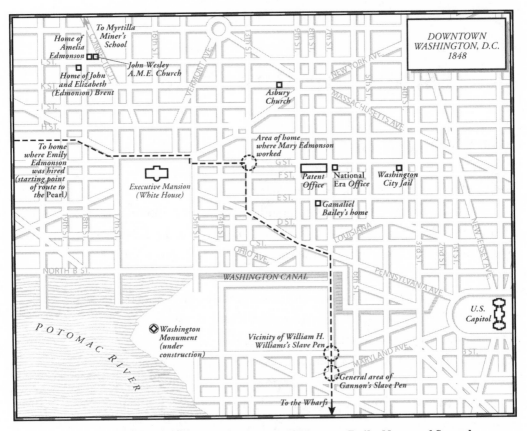

The dotted line represents the probable route Emily, Mary, and Samuel Edmonson took to get to the *Pearl*.

notice. They walked quickly, but not so fast that they appeared hurried or guilty; they preferred not to be noticed at all.

They kept a steady pace, block after block, until they approached the house at the intersection of Thirteenth and G Streets where their sister Mary worked. Emily could see her older sister standing at an upstairs window, waiting and watching for them. Mary's silhouette disappeared, and a moment later she stepped barefoot out the door. She slipped on her shoes and joined Emily and Samuel.

The three runaways made a quick stop at a bakery on F Street. Inside, Emily inhaled the yeasty, sweet aroma of freshly baked bread. A friend on the late shift sold Samuel five dozen rolls—no questions asked; then they continued on their way. Many in the black community knew about the plan, but they knew not to talk about it in public: They didn't want to risk being overheard.

A drizzly rain began to fall by the time Emily, Samuel, and Mary passed near the homes of slave trader Joseph Gannon and William H. Williams, a slave trader who ran one of the most fearsome slave pens in Washington, D.C. Williams's house looked like an ordinary residence, except for the high brick wall that surrounded the backyard. That wall hid the truth, a reality that genteel white residents of the nation's capital didn't want to see and enslaved people didn't want to be reminded of. Behind that wall, the yard was lined with prison cells, shackles, whips, and, of course, men, women, and children held in bondage to be sold as slaves. Emily knew that if she and her siblings were caught trying to escape, they could easily end up in a slave pen just like that.

It had to be well past 9 p.m. by now, dangerously close to the "colored curfew." Keep moving, keep moving. Emily listened for the sound of the bell at the Perseverance Fire Company signaling the hour. When the ten o'clock bell rang, all black people—both free and enslaved—had to be off the streets or they could be arrested, fined, and flogged or beaten.

They walked a little faster, marching down Seventh Street and across the Washington City Canal, which smelled of rotting fish and discarded produce. They hurried on in the direction of

Discrimination: A Matter of Law

If you were black and you lived in the nation's capital in 1848, you had more to worry about than simply a 10 p.m. curfew. A group of regulations known as the Black Code established a legal system of discrimination against black residents. The law, spelled out in The Black Code of the District of Columbia, stated that among other infractions, it was illegal for blacks, whether free or enslaved, to vote, hold elective office, testify against whites in court, serve on juries, own firearms, bathe in certain waters, stay out past 10 p.m., hold dances, or fly kites.

Black people who could not present documentation of their free status could be imprisoned in slave pens such as this one in Alexandria, Virginia, shown in a photo from the early 1860s.

In addition, blacks were considered enslaved unless they could document their free status. In an absurd miscarriage of justice, some free black people who did not have their papers when they were stopped were falsely accused of being slaves and imprisoned because they could not prove their status. They were then responsible for paying their jail fees; if they could not afford to pay, they were sold as slaves. One of the most notorious examples of this practice was the capture of Solomon Northup, a free man who was sold into slavery because he did not have his free papers with him. His story was documented in his 1853 autobiography, *Twelve Years a Slave*.

the Potomac River, then turned east on a secluded path toward White House Wharf, named for the single white house perched on the bluff overlooking the river. The dampness of the grass soaked her feet and weighed down the hem of her skirt as Emily crossed a field. As she approached the landing down by the river, she first saw two lights marking the bow and stern of a ship. Eventually, the fog and mist thinned enough for her to make out the shape of a two-masted vessel. That was it, her passage to freedom: the *Pearl*.

Escape on the *Pearl*

When the Edmonsons boarded the *Pearl*, they were unaware that they were about to take part in the largest and most ambitious slave escape attempt in United States history. They knew only the basic plan: The *Pearl* was to sail about 225 miles down the Potomac River and up the Chesapeake Bay to Frenchtown Wharf, Maryland. This was one of the few ports deep enough for a ship of that size to dock. After the journey on the water, which was expected to take three to five days, depending on the weather, the fugitives planned to travel to Philadelphia, most likely making the 16-mile journey along the New Castle and Frenchtown Turnpike on foot or in carriages.

The original plan had been modest in scale, but the abolitionist organizers allowed the plot to expand, ultimately inviting 77 runaways to take part. They hoped that the size and scope of the escape would draw nationwide attention to the debate over slavery in the nation's capital. At the time, the existence of slavery was a matter left to the states, but Washington, D.C., was different. Congress had the authority to abolish slavery in the District, if it chose to do so. The presence of slavery in the District of Columbia had become the center of an increasingly serious nationwide conflict between abolitionists and advocates of slavery.

BOARDING THE *PEARL*

Emily paused at the edge of the wharf, aware that when she boarded the boat she was going to change her life in ways she could not predict: She had never disobeyed her owner's wishes before; she had never broken the law before; she had never done anything so dangerous before. She drew a deep breath and moved forward.

On board, a nervous young white man flashed a lantern in Emily's face and looked her over, head to toe. Without speaking, he opened the hatch, permitting Emily and her siblings to go below deck. She glanced back toward the city, toward the life she was leaving behind, and she followed her sister and brother down a wooden ladder to the hold below.

Two small lanterns illuminated the crowded space inside the belly of the ship, leaving much of the cabin in darkness. Everywhere Emily looked she saw the anxious faces of neighbors and friends, people she knew well and some she did not recognize at all. Young and old, men, women, and children, all jammed into the small, low-ceilinged space. At five feet, two inches tall, Emily could stand straight, but the taller runaways had to crouch, since the hold had less than six feet of headroom.

A moment later, Emily saw three of her other brothers— Ephraim, Richard, and John—who waved from the back of the boat. Emily followed Samuel and Mary through the crowd, toward a small cleared space where her older brothers had placed two boxes for their sisters to sit so that they might get a little extra fresh air from the two portholes. Emily greeted her brothers and then took a seat.

There was no turning back: They were fugitives now.

Captain Drayton's Change of Heart

As a young man, Daniel Drayton had little sympathy for slaves. Enslaved people often asked him, as the captain of a small bay craft, if he would help them make their way to freedom by allowing them to board his ship as stowaways. For years, Drayton ignored their pleas. "At that time, I had regarded the negroes as only fit to be slaves," Drayton wrote in his 1853 memoir.

But Drayton's opinions about slavery changed after he converted to Christianity. "I no longer considered myself as living for myself alone," he wrote. "I regarded myself as bound to do unto others as I would that they should do to me. . . . Why had not these black people, so anxious to escape from their masters, as good a right to their liberty as I had to mine?"

Drayton first helped with a slave escape in 1847, a year before his experience with the *Pearl*. He docked a ship loaded with oysters at the Seventh Street Wharf in the District of Columbia. Not long after Drayton arrived, a free black man approached him and offered to pay him to smuggle his wife and five children to the North. The desperate man explained that his wife had already paid for her freedom but her owner refused to release her. If Drayton didn't help him, slave traders would send the man's family south and he would likely never see them again.

Drayton sympathized with the family's situation. He hid the woman and her five children and a niece onboard his ship and took them to the northern end of the Chesapeake Bay, where the woman's husband met them and escorted them to freedom in Pennsylvania, a state that had outlawed slavery. Pleased with the outcome of the first escape, Drayton agreed to repeat the plan, this time on a boat called the *Pearl*.

⇜ THREE ⇝

Against the Tide

JUDSON DIGGS, A free man of color, made his living driving passengers in his carriage. He pulled the reins and his mule, Caesar, halted down by the water just east of the Seventh Street Wharf. Diggs climbed down from the driver's seat, then helped his two female passengers exit the carriage with their bundles.

Diggs almost certainly knew that his passengers were runaway slaves. Many people in the black community had heard whispers about arrangements being made for a large-scale escape. When they were unloaded at the wharf, he asked the women for his fare: 25 cents.

The women apologized, explaining that they did not have the money, but they promised to pay him when they reached freedom.

Diggs may have sympathized with their desire for freedom, but he did not give free rides and he did not like feeling duped. Diggs did not expect to ever receive payment. Angry, he left the women at the wharf, turned toward the city, and urged his mule back up the wet and muddy path.

Sometime after ten o'clock, Emily heard the sound of shuffling feet and the noise of heavy ropes and chains dragging and dropping on the deck above. Not much later, the boat rocked gently and

This horse-drawn wagon may have been similar to the one used by Judson Diggs in 1848.

the hull creaked and groaned as the ship drifted from the wharf to the middle of the Potomac River. The *Pearl* had eased its way only about a half mile downriver when it stalled completely. Emily stared out of the small porthole, but the scenery did not change. Where was the wind?

Those below deck may have been able to hear the anchor being thrown overboard and splashing into the water. With so little wind to combat the tide, the ship needed to anchor to avoid being pushed back up the river toward Washington. At that point, they were trapped midstream, waiting for the winds to stir and the tides to change. The water was dead calm, stagnant. If the wind didn't pick up soon, the ship would be a helpless target for slave owners eager to recapture and reclaim their runaways.

Throughout the night, those on board prayed for stronger winds to complete their escape or for compassion from their captors if they made it no farther. After dawn on Sunday morning, the sun began to dissolve the fog and stir the air. They heard chains rattling on the deck as someone raised the anchor and the ship began to drift. A middle-aged white man with a thin, weathered face and long, wavy hair uncovered the hatches, allowing a rush of fresh air to flood the cabin below deck. The man distributed bread and removed the bulkhead between the hold and the cabin so that those who wanted to could get into the cabin to cook.

At last, the wind began to grow stronger and the boat hurried along, trying to make up for lost time. The sound of water sloshing against the hull and the bounce of the ship in the waves reassured those on board that they were, at last, on their way.

SUNDAY WORSHIP

No one knows what scripture was read or what prayers were shared aloud, but it is known that the runaways staged an impromptu church service in the dark cabin below deck on Sunday morning. Several people rummaged through their belongings and pulled out the Bibles that they had brought with them, and they took turns reading aloud. At home, Emily and Mary had worshiped regularly at the Asbury Methodist Church on the corner of Eleventh and K Streets, so they would have found comfort in the familiar words and affirming messages. Emily remained frightened and expected the journey to freedom to be difficult, but she believed the promise that salvation would follow their time of trial. Mary, always poised and pious, was a source of strength with her faith and steadfast belief in the Divine. Mary may have been only 15 years old, but sitting next to her made Emily feel safer.

Emily listened intently. When someone near her held out the Bible and offered to pass it to her for a turn at reading, Emily smiled and shook her head. She and Mary could neither take a turn reading aloud nor follow the words in the text because neither of them knew how to read. Instead, Emily listened and prayed—for safe passage, for steady winds, for family left behind, for freedom. She felt grateful that she and her brothers and sister and all those on board had made it through their first night as fugitives.

During the service, Emily may have thought about her mother and the family she had left behind. On the afternoon of their escape, Emily, Mary, and Samuel had visited their parents and older sisters. When it was time to say good-bye, Emily's mother had held each of her children and said, as she did each time they parted, "Be good children and the blessed Lord will take care of you." Her mother's final words were the same she always said, but those words now took on special meaning.

All around her, voices rose up, singing familiar hymns. Emily added her voice to Mary's and the others', letting the words and melodies fill the stale, dark cabin and transform it into a holy place.

The blessed Lord will take care of you. Please, yes, please.

Slavery and Literacy

Laws against educating enslaved people are older than the Declaration of Independence. As far back as 1740, the South Carolina General Assembly had enacted a law that made it illegal to teach someone in bondage to write. Writing was considered a sign of status and deemed unnecessary for black Americans, free or enslaved. Reading, on the other hand, was encouraged during the colonial period, so that slaves could become familiar with the Bible.

The watercolor "Black man reading newspaper by candlelight" was painted in 1863 by Henry Louis Stephens. The headline of the newspaper he is reading says, "Presidential Proclamation, Slavery."

The literacy laws that made it illegal for slaves to both read and write came almost 100 years later, in reaction to Nat Turner's 1831 rebellion, in which he and his supporters killed 60 white people while attempting to launch a revolution against slavery. After that event, slave owners feared that their slaves would learn to read and write passes (letters of permission for travel) and antislavery materials and that with these skills they could more easily prepare an organized uprising.

Despite the laws, some enslaved people became literate. Instruction was done in secret because in the South, those who were caught teaching black people to read could be fined, beaten, or imprisoned. Slaves learning to read were often beaten, and some had their fingers and toes amputated. Still, reading offered intellectual freedom, and for many, the desire to read and write overshadowed the risks of punishment.

FOUR

Chasing the *Pearl*

O N SUNDAY, APRIL 16, 1848, in Washington, D.C., dozens of white families woke up to find that their morning fires had not been lit, their livestock had not been fed, and their breakfast had not been prepared. Where were their slaves?

They soon learned that other owners' slaves were missing, too. Joseph Downing discovered that his slave, John Brooke, was missing; former first lady Dolley Madison's slave Mary Stewart could not be found; John Stull learned that his slave, Mary Ann, and two of her sons were gone. During the course of the morning, word of the escapes traveled from house to house; the total number of known missing slaves grew by the hour. Runaway slaves were fairly common, but they usually fled alone or in pairs or small family groups. Could scores of enslaved people have been so bold and reckless as to escape together?

There was no time to waste. Major Hampton C. Williams, justice of the peace, rang the church and fire bells, calling the men in the surrounding neighborhoods into action. Within the hour, Williams and a half dozen other men had formed a search party, mounted their horses, and started toward the roads leading north out of the city, the most common escape routes used by fleeing slaves.

Williams slowed his horse when, on the outskirts of town, he encountered Judson Diggs, the carriage driver who had been cheated out of his 25-cent fare the night before. He asked Diggs what he knew about the escape.

Diggs could have said he knew nothing. He could have encouraged the posse to explore the roads out of town or steered them onto another false path. Instead, Diggs told Williams that he and his men were headed the wrong way and to look down at the Seventh Street Wharf.

Williams sized up his informant: Could Diggs be trusted? Williams hadn't considered an escape on the water, and he wasn't confident about the accuracy of the information.

With no time to waste, Williams divided the search party, and one group continued toward the main roads while he and several others circled back toward the wharf. Williams went down to the water and learned that a schooner known as the *Pearl* had been docked there but left in the middle of the night. Williams knew that Diggs had been telling the truth.

One of the men in the posse, Francis Dodge Jr., offered the use of his steamboat so that they could continue the search on the water. Dodge, a wealthy tobacco trader from Georgetown, owned three of the runaway slaves. By noon, Williams, Dodge, and about 30 other men set out on Dodge's steamboat, the *Salem*.

Williams and his men knew that the *Pearl* had a big head start, but they didn't know how far ahead the runaways might be. The weather had turned windy, which made sea travel unsafe, but they had no choice except to ignore the approaching storm. When they met a passenger steamboat making its way north up the Potomac River, Samuel Baker, the captain of the *Salem*, flagged down the boat and asked the captain if he had seen a schooner headed down the Potomac toward the Chesapeake Bay. He learned that the *Pearl* wasn't far ahead.

ONE STEP AHEAD

By Sunday afternoon, the wind kicked up another notch. The *Pearl* began to rock and sway—back and forth, back and forth—the rhythm occasionally broken by the jolt of an unexpected wave. Emily's stomach soured and she felt cold sweat develop across her brow. Her queasy stomach left her shaky and faint. She tried to breathe steadily to calm her stomach, but the damp, stale air below deck offered no relief. Mary could not console her because she, too, suffered from seasickness.

The girls wanted to go up on deck for a breath of fresh air, but they had to wait until after sundown so that they would not be seen by passing boats. When it was finally dark enough to

The Edmonsons boarded the *Pearl*, a ship that resembled this two-masted schooner. These bay craft boats transported coal, wood, and other cargo in the waters of the Chesapeake Bay.

climb on deck, Emily was so weak from hours of illness that she could not lift herself, so her brothers had to carry her. Emily was not as tall and slender as her sister, but her brothers did not struggle to move either one of them. Once on deck, Emily breathed the fresh air and let the wind blow across her face until she began to feel like herself again.

By nightfall, the wind had gone from gusty to gale force in strength. The *Pearl* creaked and moaned as the waves thrashed it back and forth. Could the boat survive a journey on the rough waters of the Chesapeake Bay?

On the deck, two men quarreled as the wind and rain battered the *Pearl*. One argued that they should change the route and travel to Delaware by way of the outside passage in the Atlantic Ocean; the other insisted that the ship was not seaworthy and no one would ever survive the journey. At that point, some on board may have asked themselves whether it would be worse to drown at sea or return to a brutal beating and the ongoing cruelty of slavery.

They finally settled the argument and decided to anchor the *Pearl* in Cornfield Harbor, a deepwater shelter used by ships facing dangerous winds. They would go on when the winds calmed, but until then, all they could do was rest and wait out the storm.

IN THE SHADOWS

The *Salem* sped through the night, hoping to capture the *Pearl* before it entered the bay, where it would be much more difficult to find. Wind and waves rocked the steamship, which powered on through the storm.

Just after midnight, the *Salem* reached the mouth of the Potomac River, near the Chesapeake Bay. The winds whipped around the ship and limited visibility. Their 140-mile journey had

The Slave Ship, painted by Joseph Mallord William Turner (1775–1851), shows a schooner caught in a violent storm. The *Pearl* was not built to withstand the intense conditions of open waters in a storm.

ended; they could go no farther because Dodge's steamship had not been insured for travel on the more tumultuous open waters of the bay.

Williams prepared to turn back, assuming he had lost the chase. Unwilling to accept defeat, the crew continued to scan the darkness, searching for signs of the *Pearl*.

One of the men noticed something unusual near the shoreline. Was it real or a figment of his wishful thinking? The crew studied the shadows in the marshes of Cornfield Harbor and one by one they made out a shape in the darkness, a shape that looked quite a bit like the silhouette of the missing schooner.

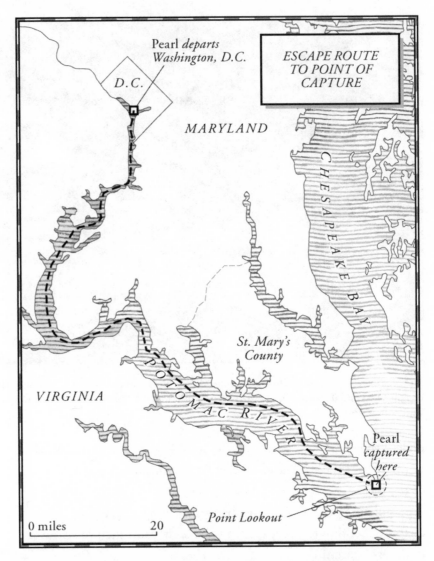

Pearl *departs*
Washington, D.C.

**ESCAPE ROUTE
TO POINT OF
CAPTURE**

D.C.

MARYLAND

CHESAPEAKE BAY

*St. Mary's
County*

VIRGINIA

POTOMAC RIVER

Pearl
*captured
here*

Point Lookout

0 miles   20

**The *Pearl* escaped down the Potomac River. The ship was captured at
Point Lookout before it was able to travel north into the Chesapeake Bay.**

⪻ FIVE ⪼

Capture

EMILY WOKE FROM a fitful sleep when she heard the whistle and hiss of a steamboat blowing off air nearby. Startled, she sat up and listened. Was that noise a trick of the wind? Or had they been discovered? She strained to hear more. A moment later, footsteps thundered on the deck above them and muffled voices mixed with the noise of the pummeling rain. No! It couldn't be. They had been free for scarcely 24 hours.

The runaways must have turned to one another, eyes wide, unsure of what to do. Mothers put their arms around their children and held them close. Some of the men searched for objects that could be used in self-defense, if necessary, but resistance would be futile; they had no guns, no knives, no weapons of any kind.

Emily and Mary joined their brothers and a group of other young fugitives to consider the essential question: Should they fight or surrender peacefully?

Samuel searched the cargo hold for something—anything—that he could use as a weapon. He found nothing suitable. He understood that he would be defeated, but the thought of being put in chains and having his sisters sent to New Orleans was too much to accept without a fight.

Emily and Richard urged Samuel to surrender peacefully to avoid bloodshed. If they fought, they would die. A moment later, an angry white man lifted the hatch and looked down at the frightened faces of the fugitives below. Emily stared up at him, unsure what to do. The cabin buzzed with frenzy and fright. Children cried and clung to their mothers' skirts; some of the women wailed, some called out for mercy, and some lowered their heads in silent defeat.

Emily watched Richard and Samuel and several of the other men bound up the stairs and onto the deck of the ship without warning. In a loud voice, Richard said, "Do yourselves no harm, gentlemen, for we are here!"

Rather than reassure the nervous posse, the sudden appearance of the muscular young runaways startled their captors. Were the men surrendering or about to put up a fight? In the rain and dim lantern light, the situation became confusing. While Emily may not have been able to discern clearly what was happening in the chaos on deck, she may have been able to see a jittery member of the posse try to throw a punch in Samuel's direction. Luckily for Samuel, at that moment, a wave crashed into the boat and the *Pearl* lurched, causing the blow to glance off the side of Samuel's head and strike someone else in the back.

Above the noise of the scuffle that followed, Emily heard the voice of the captain of the *Pearl*, urging everyone to stay calm. He pointed out that the slaves were not resisting, so there was no need for violence. No doubt the captain's appeal helped maintain peace and prevent an all-out brawl, which almost certainly would have ended in injury or death for many of the fugitives.

When order was restored, the four Edmonson brothers and the other male slaves were chained together, wrist to wrist, and moved onto the *Salem*, where they could be supervised and controlled more easily. Emily and the other women and children remained on the *Pearl*, locked below deck. They were once again enslaved, their short-lived freedom stolen from them by angry slaveholders intent on revenge.

⇜ SIX ⇝

Back to Washington

MORNING DAWNED, THE waters calmed, and the *Pearl* began its voyage back to the nation's capital, towed behind the steamship *Salem*. This time their progress proved steady and predictable, leaving the runaways plenty of opportunity to agonize over what would happen when they reached Washington, D.C.

Just after sunrise the following morning, the *Salem* arrived at Alexandria, Virginia, where Emily saw a mob of angry citizens gathered on the wharves. When the passengers were in sight of the shore, their captors ordered up on deck the white men who had helped with the escape and many of the male runaways, exhibiting them like trophies after a hunting expedition, the winnings after a day of slave-hunting as sport.

At the sight of the fugitives, the crowd went wild, yelling and cheering for their captors. If people were this worked up outside the city, what kind of angry mob would be waiting for them in Washington?

Not long after, the *Salem* docked at a steamboat wharf on the Potomac River in Washington, D.C. The passengers were forced to leave the ships in an orderly procession: first, the three white men, followed by the male slaves chained together, two by two, then the female slaves—many with babies in their arms—followed by the older children. Altogether there were 77 enslaved people: 38 men and older boys, 26 women and older girls, and 13 children.

Emily paired with Mary, of course. The two Edmonson sisters stood tall and marched toward the city with as much poise and dignity as they could muster. Each wore her long hair parted in the middle and braided into ropes that were twisted into buns. They knew they could not flee, so they trudged steadily forward, their arms around each other's waist for comfort and support.

As they made their way up Seventh Street, the crowd of spectators grew denser and more hostile. The runaways were surrounded prey in the sights of a pack of wolves, hungry for revenge. People yelled and taunted the girls as they passed. At one point someone in the mob yelled to Emily: "Aren't you ashamed to run away and make all this trouble for everybody?"

"No, sir," she replied. "We are not and if we had to go through it again, we'd do the same thing."

The man turned to the person next to him and said, "Ain't she got good spunk?"

Tears streaked the faces of many black people watching the procession, stunned and powerless, no doubt thinking about the harsh treatment that awaited the recaptured runaways. One of the faces in the crowd belonged to their brother-in-law John Brent, who watched the line of fugitives, looking for members of the family. When he saw Emily and her siblings marching toward the jail, Brent fainted; his greatest fear about the escape attempt had come to pass.

Ahead of Emily, people in the mob jeered and pushed and threatened the prisoners, especially the white men who had

The Release of Chester English

While they were being marched toward the Washington City Jail, the captain of the *Pearl*, Daniel Drayton, urged his captors to release crew member Chester English. English was a young married father, probably in his early twenties, and he had been told nothing about the escape plan. Drayton didn't want to take English on the journey in the first place, but the captain who owned the boat insisted because he had already hired English as cook and crew, and he wanted to keep him.

Drayton told English that they would be transporting a load of timber to the nation's capital. On their way to Washington they did, in fact, stop in Machodock, Virginia, to buy about 20 cords of wood, but that was not the purpose of their journey. On the night of the escape, Drayton said that a number of black people planned to join them for a trip down the bay, and that all English had to do was lift up the hatch and let them enter the hold. English was baffled by the instructions, but he promised to do what he was told. According to Drayton, English never understood that the passengers were escaping; he thought they were going on a pleasure cruise.

English had not been charged with a crime and it was clear that he was confused about what was happening. When it came time to move Drayton and the other white man into the carriage to get them away from the surrounding mob, one of the police officers released English.

Once freed, English turned and walked through the crowd, all but unnoticed. He wandered back down to the steamboat wharf, the only landmark he recognized in the city. When he arrived, the steamer *Salem* was gone.

Alone in a strange place, English was not sure what to do. Before his voyage on the *Pearl*, he had never been more than 30 miles from his home in Philadelphia. He approached a man near the wharf and rather than simply asking for help returning home, he told his entire story, including information about helping the runaways on the *Pearl*. In response, the stranger secured him in a hack and sent him back to the jail. English remained imprisoned there until the trials were held, when charges against him were dropped in exchange for his testimony against Drayton and Edward Sayres, the second captain of the *Pearl*.

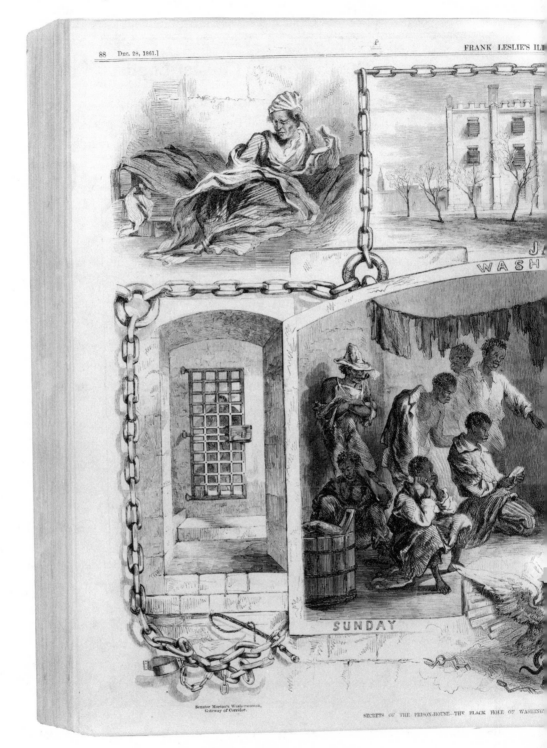

Senator Morton's Washerwoman,
Gateway of Corridor.

SECRETS OF THE PRISON-HOUSE.—THE BLACK HOLE OF WASHING

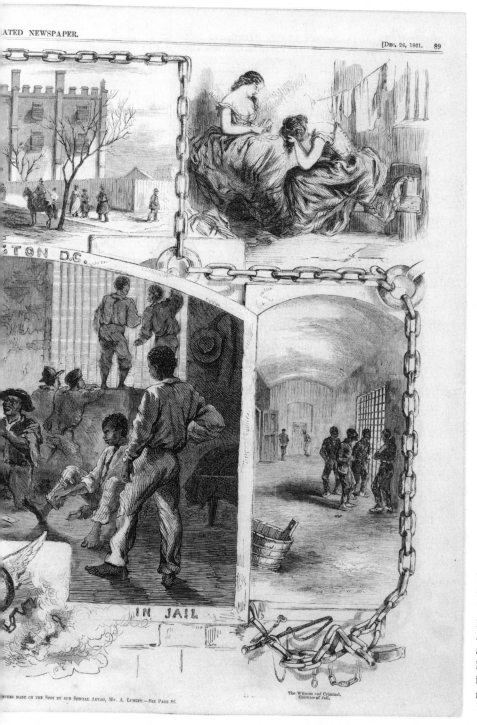

TON D.C.

IN JAIL

TCHES MADE ON THE SPOT BY OUR SPECIAL ARTIST, MR. A. LUMLEY.—SEE PAGE 84.

The Witness and Criminal,
Corridor of Jail.

This wood engraving titled "Secrets of the prison-house" by Arthur Lumley appeared in Frank Leslie's illustrated newspaper in 1861.

helped with the escape. Members of the posse flanked them as human shields, holding back the hostile crowd. Their captors had become their guardians, their only defense against assault from the irate mob.

As the prisoners marched, the size of the mob continued to increase. When they passed Joseph Gannon's slave pen—the same pen they had passed on the first night of their escape—the slave trader, armed with a bowie knife, rushed out, reached around the police escorts, and stabbed in the direction of one of the white captains. The blade nicked the captain's ear, causing blood to run down the man's neck as he continued to march toward the jail.

A lawman told the slave trader that the captain was in the hands of the law.

"Damn the law!" Gannon said. "I have three Negroes and I will give them all for one thrust at this scoundrel!"

The procession kept moving forward, and he followed, waiting for an opportunity to attack again. Eventually, the would-be attacker fell back in the crowd, but there were plenty of others to yell and wave fists in his place.

By this time, the crowd had grown to several thousand people. When the prisoners had almost reached Pennsylvania Avenue, the mob began to chant: "Lynch them! Lynch them!"

The lawmen had lost control of the crowd. If the mob moved to hang the accused, nothing could be done to stop them. Not long after, one of the police officers hired a carriage and shoved the white men into it. The mob surrounded the carriage and followed as it made its way toward the jail. The white men were safer in jail than they would have been on the street.

BEHIND BARS

Emily and the other runaways kept marching and eventually arrived at the Washington City Jail, more commonly known as the Blue Jug because of the garish shade of blue paint covering the three-story stone building with iron bars on the windows. When they arrived at the jail, most of the fugitives were forced into the cold, damp basement cells, but Emily and Mary were directed to the women's quarters upstairs. Their cell had no bed or chairs or other furnishings, just a single blanket to protect them from the hard, cold floor, but they found comfort in being together.

The haunting and mournful voices and cries of the prisoners bounced off the walls. Although they had been enslaved all their lives, until they heard the clang of the cell door lock behind them that day, Emily and Mary had never been caged.

The Abolitionist Press

Abolitionists used the press to change public opinion and promote their antislavery agenda. Starting around 1820, abolitionists published a steady stream of newspapers, children's books, sermons, speeches, broadsides, memoirs of former slaves, and other documents that helped to present their case. In the mid-19th century, more than 40 newspapers promoted the emancipation of slaves, including William Lloyd Garrison's *The Liberator* (1831–1865), Frederick Douglass's *North Star* (1838–1851), and the *National Anti-Slavery Standard* (1840–1870), the official newspaper of the American Anti-Slavery Society.

Showdown at the *National Era*

On the day the fugitives from the *Pearl* marched through Washington, D.C., the mob followed them all the way to the front of the Washington City Jail. After the prisoners were secured inside, the mob continued to grow. Someone suggested that they move several blocks down the street to the office of the *National Era*, an antislavery newspaper edited by abolitionist Gamaliel Bailey. No one in the crowd had any evidence that the newspaper had anything to do with the escape on the *Pearl*, but many of the protesters assumed that the press and its editor were at least sympathetic to the cause.

Gamaliel Bailey (1807–1859) used journalism to promote the abolitionist cause. Before editing the *National Era*, he worked at the Cincinnati *Philanthropist*, the first antislavery newspaper in the west.

The mob moved down the street to the newspaper building across from the U.S. Patent Office, on Seventh Street. As the evening wore on, the crowd became increasingly excited and belligerent—louder, bigger, angrier. At one point, someone picked up a stone and hurled it toward the building. Someone else grabbed a brick and broke a window and a door, adding the sound of shattering glass to the din of the night.

Captain John H. Goddard, a leader in the city's Auxiliary Guard, tried to calm the crowd, attempting to convince the agitators that they didn't want to give the sympathizers in the North any more reason to become involved in District business.

Someone else in the crowd defended the right of a free press, even an abolitionist press.

The mob had reached a pivotal moment—that turning point at which it must decide whether to press on with violence or settle down and act with civility. Suddenly, a strong wind stirred and brought with it an unexpected downpour. The energy shifted; the rain dampened the enthusiasm of the rioters. The crowd cleared around ten o'clock, but not before agreeing to meet again the following night.

The second night, a crowd of several thousand people, most from Maryland and Virginia rather than the District, gathered once again outside the *National Era* building, threatening to destroy the press and run its editor, 40-year-old Gamaliel Bailey, out of town. From the steps of the Patent Office, across from the *Era*, Daniel Radcliffe, a prominent Washington lawyer, tried to convince the members of the crowd to go home, but they grew more agitated. When it became clear that the crowd would not leave without some action, Radcliffe negotiated a compromise in which a committee of 50, five men from each ward in the city plus Georgetown and Tenleytown, agreed to present their case to Bailey.

Members of the committee assembled outside Bailey's home, a block away from the *Era* offices. The newspaper editor opened his door and stood on his front porch to address the crowd. A spokesman for the group tried to convince Bailey to shut down the press voluntarily: "This community is satisfied that the existence of your press among us is endangering the public peace." He told Bailey that he had until 10 a.m. the following day to close the *Era* or face the consequences.

Bailey listened to his critics' complaints. He could hear the shouting and chanting of the angry crowd a block away. When the members of the committee finished, Bailey addressed the mob: "Let me say to you that I am a peace-man. I have taken no measures to defend my office, my house or myself. I appeal to the good sense and intelligence of the community, and stand upon my rights as an American citizen, looking to the law alone for protection."

The protesters urged him to reconsider his position: "We advise you to be out of the way! The people think that your press endangers their property and their lives; and they have appointed us to tell you so, and ask you to remove it tomorrow. If you say that you will do so, they will retire satisfied. If you refuse, they say they will tear it down."

The discussion continued, but they had reached an impasse.

Finally, Bailey, whose previous abolitionist press had been destroyed three times by mob violence, said: "I cannot surrender my rights. Were I to die for it, I cannot surrender my rights! Tell those who sent you hither

This 1859 photograph shows the view from the *National Era* building, including the front of the U.S. Patent Office Building on Seventh Street and the U.S. Post Office on the right. The angry mob gathered in the open space, and those addressing the crowd stood on the stairs of the Patent Office in front of the pillars.

that my press and my house are undefended. They must do as they see proper. I maintain my rights and I make no resistance!"

Bailey went inside his home and closed the door.

Outside, the crowd chanted, "Down with the *Era!*" "Gut the office!"

The mob retreated and regrouped at the newspaper offices a block away. Once they left, Bailey woke his six young children and moved them to the safety of his next-door neighbor's house just in case the protesters returned to attack his home and family.

When the gang arrived at the *Era* offices, they found that city police had been stationed to guard the building. Rather than challenging the officers, the mob passed a resolution "to pull it down the next day at ten o'clock if the press was not meanwhile removed."

In the morning, ten o'clock came—and went—without violence. The press remained intact and Bailey published the regular weekly edition of the *National Era*. In it he described the attacks against him, calling them an outrage against freedom. He also denied any involvement in the escape on the *Pearl* and pledged that he would never "take part in any movement that would involve treachery of any kind."

Other newspapers also called for an end to the violence. On April 20, 1848, the board of aldermen and Auxiliary Guard published handbills promoting peace and stating that "events have transpired within the last few days deeply affecting the peace and character of our community." The notices warned that "fearful acts of lawless and irresponsible violence can only aggregate the evil."

Whether the crowds found the arguments persuasive or they lost interest in the cause can't be known, but after three days of turmoil and tension, the city grew quiet again.

SEVEN

Sold

AFTER A RESTLESS night in jail, Emily, Mary, and the other runaways were taken downstairs. The justices of the peace called the prisoners forward one by one so that they could be identified by their owners and reclaimed. Some of the runaways stared at the floor in submission; others looked at their captors with contempt. Some wept; others stood silent, resigned to their future and too physically and emotionally exhausted to protest.

During the proceedings, Emily listened as one female slave who tried to run away with her child was given the chance to repent and return to her owner rather than risk being sold south. She refused. When a newspaper reporter covering the event asked the woman why she had rejected her owner's offer, she said: "Have I not the same right to my freedom that you have, and could you have neglected a chance of gaining it had you been a slave?"

Moments later, another woman stepped forward when she heard her name called and said: "Here I am, sir, once free, again a slave."

Emily recognized Valdenar, the man who managed Culver's business affairs. When their names were called by the judge, Emily and the other Edmonson runaways stepped forward. As they passed the two white captains, one of the girls (probably Mary) said: "God bless you, sirs. You did all you could. It is not your fault that we are not free."

Valdenar did not take the Edmonsons with him. Instead, he went outside the jail to speak with the slave dealers who had come to negotiate with owners who were willing to sell their runaways at a discount rather than take the chance that they would escape again. How much could he get if he sold all six of the Edmonsons on the spot?

Acting on behalf of the family, John Brent, Elizabeth's husband, came down to the jail and asked Valdenar what it would cost to buy his family's freedom. Brent explained to Valdenar that he did not have all the money he needed on hand, but he begged the agent to give him time to raise the necessary funds from sympathetic family and friends.

The cost to buy six slaves was enormous. Strong, able-bodied men and youthful, attractive women—especially those like Emily and Mary with pale complexions—routinely sold for $800 to $1,000 apiece, sometimes more. Paul Edmonson, father of the runaways, was freed when his owner died and emancipated him in her will, and he worked to save money to buy a 40-acre farm in Montgomery County. He grew oats, corn, and potatoes; he also owned several cows, pigs, and horses. If he sold everything he had, the farm and everything on it, he would not have enough money to buy back a *single one* of his children.

Valdenar considered the offer and told Brent that he could have one day, 24 hours, to raise a good-faith deposit. Brent hurried away, grateful for the chance to ransom his family but daunted by the task that lay ahead.

The following morning, Brent went to Valdenar's home to negotiate a final price. Instead of naming a figure, Valdenar told Brent that he had already sold the six Edmonson siblings to Bruin & Hill, slave dealers from Alexandria and Baltimore, for $4,500.

It would do no good for Brent to protest; the sale had been

completed. Now that a slave dealer was involved, the price would be even higher, making it much more difficult to ransom them. How could he ever raise enough money to buy their freedom?

Although the cause seemed hopeless, Brent went to Alexandria, Virginia, to beg the slave trader, 39-year-old Joseph Bruin, to let him buy back his wife's brothers and sisters. Bruin refused to consider selling them, explaining that he had had his eyes on the family for years and could get twice what he had paid for them in the New Orleans market. Brent's pleading had no impact on Bruin. Hopeless and distraught, Brent had to leave, knowing he might never see Emily and the other runaway members of his family again.

INTO THE NIGHT

Back at the jail, Emily watched in anguish as, all around her, families were being destroyed, divided, and sold apart: Children were torn from their parents, wives from their husbands, brothers from their sisters.

Emily and Mary returned to their jail cell, uncertain of their fate. Emily could not imagine being forced to go on without her family, especially her beloved sister. She tried to settle in for the night, turning and shifting position until she made herself as comfortable as possible on the stone floor. She heard Mary breathing next to her, slow and steady. Not much later, one of the jailers appeared outside the cell and told the girls to get up and follow him. It was past ten o'clock. Why would they be asked to move in the middle of the night?

Emily looked at Mary. She could not help but hope that members of their family had been able to come up with the money necessary to buy their freedom. Were they being sent home to their mother's house, no longer enslaved but free?

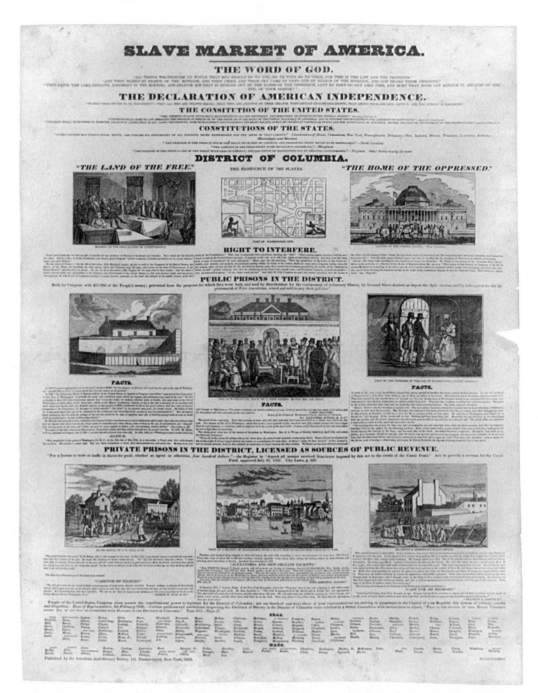

This broadside was produced as part of a petition campaign to convince Congress to outlaw slavery in the nation's capital. The text and images portray the horrors and injustice of slavery. The text notes that on February 8, 1836, the House of Representatives rejected the petition to abolish slavery in Washington, D.C., by a vote of 163 to 47.

Trying not to wake the others resting in their cells, Emily and Mary went down the stone staircase to the main level of the jail. Their hopes of liberty were lost as soon as they saw their four brothers, their wrists bound by handcuffs.

Outside the jail, they were loaded into a carriage and taken through the streets of the sleeping city, across the bridge to Alexandria, Virginia. The horses slowed and the carriage stopped at 1707 Duke Street. From the road, the building looked like a comfortable Federal-style brick home, but the high walls around the yard revealed the truth: They had arrived at a slave pen.

CAPTIVE AT BRUIN & HILL

Once they were in the backyard, Emily and Mary were separated from their brothers and taken to a large, dark cell without a bed or blanket. Emily could hear the sounds of the night—sleeping, snoring, stirring in the darkness—but she was unsure how many other people were held in the surrounding cells. Emily tried to keep quiet and settle down for the few hours of quiet before morning; she was exhausted and afraid, and she knew it would do no good to make noise now.

In the morning, Emily saw her brothers eating breakfast and learned that the men were kept together in a lower-level cell. She and Mary were assigned the unpleasant jobs of dumping and cleaning out the chamber pots and doing the laundry for the 13 men also held at Bruin & Hill.

She learned that Bruin had said that he would not sell any of the Edmonsons, but it was understood that he would do so if enough money was offered. Time was the enemy: Family and friends were collecting money for the girls' ransom, but where would they find the nearly $5,000 needed to prevent a trip to the New Orleans market?

The 1861 photograph shows a slave pen in Alexandria, Virginia, similar to Bruin & Hill.

Samuel wept and apologized to his sisters, begging them to forgive him for leading them into trouble. He said that he would gladly die for them, if that would save them from the fate he feared. Emily tried to reassure her brother and put his heart at peace, but there was nothing any of them could do but wait and pray.

As the days wore on, Bruin moved Emily and Mary inside his house to work as housekeepers and babysitters. Bruin told Emily that he admired her family; they stood tall, spoke gently, and enjoyed a confidence exhibited by few others in his pen. They were poised, proud, and pious. Bruin observed that they had clearly been raised in a home that promoted strong moral and religious values.

Although he was a slave trader, Bruin made an effort to present himself as an honorable and upstanding businessman and gentleman, even to the men and women who were considered his property. Bruin waited days and then weeks to see if the Edmonson family could raise the money necessary for their ransom. If they did, he could avoid the expense and risk of sending them south. Profits to be made selling slaves were higher in the South, but so was the risk of losing his valuable property to disease.

The longer the Edmonsons stayed in Virginia, the less likely it was that they would be sent south. In late May, the slave-trading "season" in New Orleans ended, because traders didn't want to expose their property to yellow fever and other infectious diseases, which were widespread in the hot, mosquito-filled summer months. By late April, with the end of the slave-selling season fast approaching, Bruin wanted to sell the Edmonsons quickly, either to the family or to the highest bidder in the South.

Bruin had met with Paul Edmonson, but Paul was unable to come up with the money to ransom his children. They were out of time.

Since the family had not been able to come up with any money, Bruin made up his mind: As soon as possible he would send the six Edmonson runaways, along with about 40 other enslaved people, by steamship to Baltimore, where they would catch a second ship to New Orleans.

What Happened to Judson Diggs?

In the days that followed the capture of the *Pearl*, the families of the runaways tried to figure out how the plot had been discovered. No one knows how Judson Diggs's betrayal was revealed, but members of the black community blamed him for the failed plan. Diggs was one of them—he knew the sting of slavery and the satisfaction of finding freedom—so many considered his act of denying liberty to others to be unforgivable.

Taking the law into their own hands, a group of young black men sought revenge by pulling Diggs from his carriage, beating him up, and throwing him into a stream that ran along the north side of the old John Wesley Church in Washington, D.C. Diggs survived and fully recovered from his physical injuries. He was considered an outcast—"despised and avoided"—until he died in his late sixties.

EIGHT

Baltimore

WHEN THEY ARRIVED in Baltimore, Emily, Mary, and about a dozen other enslaved people walked from the steamboat landing to 11 Camden Street, a slave pen run by Joseph S. Donovan, a partner of Bruin & Hill. At first, Emily found the slave trader's unapologetically crass and vulgar language startling, but she did her best not to listen to his profanity or obscene and insulting remarks, especially those targeting the female slaves.

Emily forced herself to tolerate his rudeness, but when he forbade the women to pray together, she and Mary decided to disobey. They began waking up very early in the morning so that they could meet with four or five other women and worship without interruption. The girls were devout Methodists; their faith defined who they were and they refused to abandon their religion to appease a godless slave trader.

Other women joined in their prayer circle, including one known as Aunt Rachel, a middle-aged woman with a strong faith who had been sold away from her husband. Emily's heart ached when she heard Aunt Rachel tell how her poor husband often used to come to the prison and beg the trader to sell her to his owners, who he thought were willing to purchase her, if the price was not too high.

The trader repeatedly ran him off the lot with brutal threats and curses.

Emily longed for her parents and family back in Washington; she understood Aunt Rachel's sorrow. Most enslaved people knew that sorrow, either from experience or from the threat of losing a loved one. Emily prayed for Aunt Rachel to be reunited with her husband and for their ultimate freedom. That was all she could do, and she would not allow a vicious slave trader to stop her from making her appeal to God.

Of course, they prayed for their ransom, but this prayer seemed to go unanswered. Emily and her siblings were told to pack their things and prepare to leave for New Orleans. The day before they were to sail out of Baltimore Harbor, they finally received word that a messenger would arrive on the morning train, ready to negotiate with the slave trader for the purchase of the family. All night, Emily dreamed that she was just hours away from freedom. She imagined that the messenger would arrive, cash in hand, ready to take them home to Washington as free women.

In the morning, Joseph Donovan forced Emily and the others to march down to the wharf. They begged for more time: Their representative was on his way, but his train would not arrive for another hour.

The slave trader felt he had waited long enough. Apparently unconcerned about the Edmonsons' plight, he had the crew of the *Union* continue to get ready for their departure. Once the Edmonsons boarded the ship, a two-masted, square-rigged brig, there was little chance that they would ever return or see their family again.

LAST-MINUTE NEGOTIATIONS

Emily waited aboard the *Union*, unaware that on shore the train from Washington had arrived. William Chaplin, a well-dressed, 52-year-old Harvard-educated abolitionist, arrived at the slave pen as a representative of the Edmonson family. Donovan soon learned that Chaplin had with him only $900, a great deal of money, but not nearly enough to buy all six family members. Chaplin wanted to use the cash—donated by a grandson of John Jacob Astor, a German-American businessman who had made a fortune in the fur trade—as a down payment on all six of the Edmonsons, but the slave trader refused.

Instead, after some discussion, Donovan said that he would consider selling one of the men, but he refused to sell the girls at any price. Chaplin pressed for a more advantageous arrangement, but ultimately he agreed to buy Richard Edmonson, whose wife and children were said to be suffering without him. Chaplin handed over the $900 in exchange for the paperwork granting Richard his freedom.

By the time they had finished their business, the inspector of the Port of Baltimore had already checked over the Manifest of Negroes, Mulattos, and Persons of Color. In that document, Mary was listed as 17 and Emily as 15; their ages were increased to make them more desirable to men in the New Orleans market. The *Union* had pulled away from the wharf. The slave trader refused to call back the ship to allow Richard to disembark. Even though he was a free man, Richard would have to sail to New Orleans, then sail back to Washington to rejoin his family at some future date. When the *Union* drifted out of Baltimore's Inner Harbor, Richard had no idea that he was, in fact, free.

What Happened to the Other Fugitives of the *Pearl*?

H ope Slatter, a slave trader from Baltimore, bought most of the fugitives from the *Pearl*. At sunset on the Friday after the escape, Slatter marched nearly 50 people through the streets of Washington, D.C., to the Baltimore and Ohio railroad depot, where they were to be sent to the southern slave market. The following letter, published in several northern newspapers, provides an eyewitness account of the events that evening:

Washington, April 22, 1848

Last evening, as I was passing the railroad depot, I saw a large number of colored people gathered round one of the cars, and from manifestations of grief among some of them, I was induced to draw near and ascertain the cause of it. I found in the car towards which they were so eagerly gazing about fifty color [*sic*] people, some of whom were nearly as white as myself. . . . About half of them were females, a few of whom had but a slight tinge of African blood in their veins, and were finely formed and beautiful. The men were ironed together, and the whole group looked sad and dejected. At each end of the car stood two ruffianly-looking personages, with large canes in their hands, and, if their countenances were an index of their hearts, they were the very impersonation of hardened villainy itself.

In the middle of the car stood the notorious slave dealer of Baltimore, Slatter, who . . . had purchased the men and women around him and was taking his departure for Georgia. While observing this old, gray-headed villain—this dealer in the bodies and souls of men—the chaplain of the Senate [Chaplain Henry Slicer] entered the car and took his brother Slatter by the hand, chatted with him for some time and seemed to view the heart-rending scene before him with as little concern as we should look upon cattle. . . .

Some of the colored people outside, as well as in the car, were weeping most bitterly. I learned that many families were separated. Wives were there to take leave of their husbands, and husbands of their wives, children of their parents, brothers and sisters shaking hands perhaps for the last time, friends parting with friends, and the tenderest ties of humanity sundered at the single bid of the inhuman slave broker before them. A husband, in the meridian of life, begged to see the partner of his bosom. He protested that she was free—that she had free papers and was torn from him and shut up in the jail. He clambered up to one of the windows of the car to see his wife, and, as she was reaching forward her hand to him, the black-hearted villain, Slatter, ordered him down. He did not obey. The husband and wife, with tears streaming down their cheeks, besought him to let them converse for a moment.

But no! A monster more hideous, hardened and savage, than the blackest spirit of the pit, knocked them down from the car and ordered him away. The bystanders could hardly restrain themselves from laying violent hands upon the brutes. This is but a faint description of that scene, which took place within a few rods of the capitol, under enactments recognized by Congress. O! what a revolting scene to a feeling heart.

—John Slingerland, Albany, New York

MANIFEST of NEGROES, MULATTOS, and PERSONS OF COLOR, taken on board the *Brig Alo —* whereof *Janus Fooks* is Master, burthen 2 3 6 tons, to be transported to the port of *Mobile —* in the district of *Alabama —* for the purpose of being sold or disposed of as slaves, or to be held to service or labor.

NUMBER OF ENTRY.	NAMES.	SEX.		AGE.	HEIGHT.		Whether Negro, Mulatto, or Person of Color.	OWNER OR SHIPPER'S	
		MALE.	FEMALE.		FEET.	INCHES.		NAME.	RESIDENCE.
1	Hinson Thomas	"		45	5	9	Black	B McCampbell	Baltimore
2	Charly Hopkins	"		23	5	11	"		
3	Samuel Matthews	"		40	5	10	Mulatto		
4	George Brooks	"		18	5	10½	Do		
5	Elisha Trout	"		20	5	10	Black		
6	Joseph Roach	"		23	5	7½	"		
7	Eli Jordan	"		30	5	8	"		
8	William Ross	"		20	5	6	"		
9	Nicolas Simms	"		19	5	7	Mulatto		
10	Edward Woods	"		45	5	6	Brown		
11	George Neil	"		26	5	5	Black		
12	Peter Rance	"		25	5	4	Do		
13	Daniel Best	"		22	5	4	Mulatto		
14	Frank Harrison	"		18	5	6½	Black		
15	Charles Smith	"		18	5	5	"		
16	Aaron Harrison	"		17	5	6	"		
17	William Thomas	"		22	5	3	"		
18	Aaron Joy	"		20	5	3½	"		
19	George W Curtis	"		19	5	3½	Brown		
20	John Stewart	"		17	5	3	"		
21	Aaron Hawkins	"		14	4	8	Black		
22	John Campbell	"		11	4	6	"		
23	Lorenzo Hopkins	"		10	4	2	"		
24	William Tell	"		8	3	10	"		
25	John Little	"		5	3	4	"		
26	Sarah Robinson + Child		"	25	5	3	"		
27	Jane Anderson		"	20	5	2	Brown		
28	Mary Gray		"	18	5	5	Black		
29	Jane Hawkins		"	20	5	8	Mulatto		
30	Celia Leinburger		"	17	5	5	Brown		
31	Leah Clark + Child		"	28	5	3	Black		
32	Mary Hopewell + Child		"	20	5	4	"		
33	Jane Joy + Child		"	20	5	3	"		
34	Fanny Hinson + Child		"	22	5	2	"		
35	Louisa Elliott		"	18	5	1	Mulatto		
36	Dicey Buxton		"	34	4	11½	Brown		
37	Alice Butler + Child		"	27	4	11	Black		
38	Phillis Chester		"	22	5	1½	"		
39	Dolly Martin		"	20	4	11½	"		
40	Charlotte Green		"	11	4	7	"		
41	Rachael Griggs		"	11	4	7	"		
42	Sarah Brown		"	11	4	6	"		

District of Baltimore, Port of Baltimore,   day of   184

B McCampbell Shipper of the persons named, and particularly described in the *above* manifest of *Slaves* Janus Fooks Master of the *Brig Alo —* do solemnly, sincerely, and truly swear, each of us to the best of our knowledge and belief that *the above named Slaves* have not been imported into the United State since the first day of January, one thousand eight hundred and eight; and that under the Laws of the State of Maryland *are* held to service or labor as Slaves and are not entitled to freedom under these laws, at a certain time and after a known period of service.—SO HELP GOD.

Sworn to this 4 day of *Octr* 184 before   B M. Campbell
N. F. Williams COLLECTOR.   Jo Fooks

This manifest is similar to the Manifest of Negroes, Mulattos, and Persons of Color used to document the enslaved people aboard the *Union*.

Sold South: The Second Middle Passage

The United States had an uncomfortable relationship with slavery from its earliest days. As early as the Constitutional Convention of 1787, legislators disagreed about the question of whether slavery should be allowed. As part of a compromise to keep the young country united, Congress agreed to phase out the international slave trade after 20 years. As of January 1, 1808, it became illegal to import slaves from overseas, although it remained legal to buy and sell enslaved people already in the country.

At the same time that Congress banned the transatlantic slave trade, there was an increase in demand for slave labor in the South. The Louisiana Purchase of 1803 expanded the land available for agricultural development, and

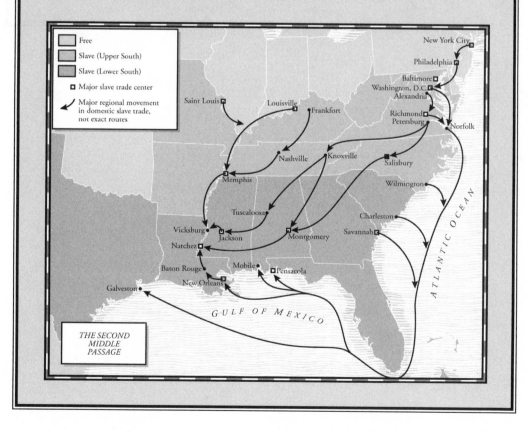

cotton and sugar, two of the most popular crops, were also very labor intensive. While there were too few slaves in the Lower South, there were too many in the Upper South. Maryland and Virginia had a surplus of slaves because of natural population increases and because farmers were planting their fields with wheat and other crops that required less labor to produce.

The result: a domestic slave trade from the Upper South to the Lower South that became known as the Second Middle Passage. (The original Middle Passage involved the transportation of enslaved people from Africa to North America.) At least one million slaves, including six members of the Edmonson family, were part of this forced migration between 1790 and 1860.

⤳ NINE ⤳

New Orleans

ONCE AGAIN, EMILY and the others sent south had to endure travel in the dark, poorly ventilated spaces below deck, in the cargo hold of the *Union*. And, not surprisingly, once again Emily and Mary suffered from severe seasickness, this time much worse than the episode on the *Pearl*. By the time the *Union* reached the Carolina coast, the winds had begun to gust from the south, pounding and rocking the ship in the ocean waves. Emily could not keep fluids down and her lips became dry and cracked. She was dangerously dehydrated, her skin wrinkled like crumpled paper, her eyes sunken into their sockets. Her breathing grew fast and shallow. Mary's condition was not much better.

How long could they hold on like that? Their brothers carried them up on deck for fresh air whenever they could do so safely, but most of the time they could do little more than sit with Emily and Mary, wipe their faces, and tell them that things were going to get better. In time, the situation did improve: The winds died down and the girls began to recover. They remained weak, but they were able to hold down fluids, giving their bodies the chance to regain strength.

Emily and the other people aboard the *Union* faced another challenge when they reached the dangerously shallow waters around Key West, Florida. Unfamiliar with the sandbars, reefs, and other hazards hidden just beneath the surface of the water, the captain of the *Union* raised a flag to signal a pilot-boat captain to guide them through the area. Before the smaller boat approached, the captain of the *Union* hid the slaves below deck, perhaps thinking that he could negotiate a lower fee if the other captain didn't know about the valuable cargo he was carrying. To conceal the slaves, the captain placed a heavy canvas cover over the grated hatchway door, blocking the air circulation in the overheated, stuffy cargo hold below.

It did not take long for the air to grow stagnant and stale. Emily felt faint and struggled to breathe while the captain and pilot up on deck squabbled about the price. The men and women had been separated into two cargo areas. One of the men took a stick and punctured a hole through the canvas on their side, introducing some fresh air. The women were unable to break the seal; they shouted for help, but no one responded. Emily breathed the hot, used air, but she was growing weaker by the minute.

After what felt like enough time to sail all the way around the world, a member of the crew pulled back the canvas, allowing air back into the hold below deck. Emily gasped to fill her lungs with as much air as they could hold. Then, one after another, as they caught their breath, the captives began to crawl out onto the deck. When they could safely move to the fresh air, Mary and Emily were too weak to stand, so once again their brothers had to carry them into the open.

The captains had not been able to agree on terms, so the pilot-boat captain refused to help them. Without a guide, the captain of the *Union* could not navigate the treacherous waters, so he had to turn back and sail the long way around Key West to remain in safer waters. That, along with foul weather, extended the length of the trip by several days. As a result, supplies of food and water began to run low. The captain rationed water, providing the crew with one quart of water a day and limiting the enslaved to just a gill a day, or about five ounces each. Emily sipped her ration slowly, but when she finished, her mouth still felt dry. She tried to deny her thirst, but she longed for fresh water. In an expression of kindness, some of the sailors shared a pint of their water supply with Emily and Mary, who, in turn, shared with the other women.

When the *Union* finally approached New Orleans on June 14, 1848, the weather turned against them again. As they arrived at the mouth of the Mississippi River, another violent storm battered the ship. The waves rolled the ship so severely that when a pilot boat approached to guide them on the journey upriver to New Orleans, it would sometimes disappear from sight as if swallowed by the waves, only to rise up and appear again when the wave passed by. Emily may have feared what awaited them in the South, but she was grateful to reach land after an exhausting 20-day journey.

TO THE SHOWROOM

The following morning, at about ten o'clock, Emily and the other 34 enslaved people left the *Union* and walked about six blocks through the city to a slave pen run by another partner of Bruin & Hill. Trembling and terrified, Emily began to cry. Without warning, an overseer approached and struck her on the chin, saying: "Stop crying or I'll give you something to cry about." He followed with another threat: "There is the calaboose [a public place for flogging slaves], where they whip those who do not behave themselves!"

As soon as the man stepped away, a woman she did not know whispered to Emily that she needed to force herself to look as cheerful as possible or she would be beaten. Emily wondered if she would ever be able to master such a false face. One of her brothers approached a moment later and asked what the woman had said; when she told him, he encouraged Emily to follow the advice.

Later that afternoon, Emily watched as her brothers were taken away. When she saw them a few hours later, she barely recognized them: Their hair had been cut short, their mustaches shaved off, and their fine butler's clothing had been exchanged for blue jackets and pants made of coarse fabric, the clothing of field slaves. Not long afterward, an overseer presented Emily and Mary with their uniforms—plain calico-print dresses and kerchiefs for their hair.

Detail from an illustration, "Slaves for Sale: A Scene in New Orleans," published in *The Illustrated London News* April 6, 1861. *Harper's Weekly* printed it with the title "A Slave Pen at New Orleans Before the Auction" on January 24, 1863.

Once they had been properly outfitted, some of the slaves were forced to stand on an open porch facing the street and display themselves to people walking by. The porch served as a store window—an outdoor show-room—and they were the merchandise. Emily and the others waited inside; and when buyers called, they paraded across the auction floor in rows. Emily tried to smile and look pleasant, but there was no joy in her expression. Some of the men in the crowd told vulgar jokes and taunted the girls as they passed, but Emily had figured out that she had to tolerate and ignore their behavior.

A man took a liking to one of the girls near Emily. He called the girl to him, then demanded that she open her mouth so that he could look at her teeth, as if he were inspecting livestock. He touched her as he pleased, and the young girl had to stand and bear it without resistance.

While no one knows the details of what Emily and Mary were forced to endure in the showroom, in many cases prospective buyers took slaves into back rooms for a closer, private inspection. A buyer interested in purchasing a particular slave could make a detailed examination of the property, demanding that male slaves take off all their clothes and females strip to the waist. Buyers looked for scars and signs of beatings, which could indicate a slave's defiant nature or a history of misbehavior. Some buyers also took advantage of the opportunity to molest or shame a girl or young woman who could not defend herself.

Watching a girl near her being manhandled, Emily burned with humiliation and anger. How could one person treat another with so little dignity? Of course, Emily knew that when she was chosen, she, too, would have to accept such treatment without complaint in order to avoid beatings—or worse.

Unfortunately, it wasn't long before an interested buyer came to the slave trader and asked for a young, attractive girl to hire as a housekeeper. The trader called for Emily.

Emily stepped forward, trembling. Fear and outrage left her cold and hollow. Surely no one would want her; she was just a girl. She could not be taken. She did not know what she would do without her sister. She tried to appear cheerful, but her chin quivered and tears slipped down her cheeks. The buyer looked her over and dismissed her. He told the slave trader that he refused to consider buying Emily because he had "no room for the snuffles in his house."

Once they were off the porch and out of view of the buyers, the trader slapped Emily across the face, hard. Her tears had lost him a $1,500 sale. He warned her that there would be worse if she didn't stop crying and look pleasant and willing in front of future customers.

Shades of Black

In addition to physical and emotional abuse, many female slaves were sexually abused by their owners and by other men they encountered in positions of power. Since they were considered property, enslaved women had no legal defense or recourse if they were raped or sexually molested. As a result, many black slaves gave birth to mixed-race children.

By law, any child of an enslaved mother was legally a slave, regardless of the legal status of the father. This practice resulted in several race classifications:

- *Mulatto* referred to a person with one black and one white parent; the word is derived from the Spanish word *mula*, meaning mule.
- *Quadroon* referred to a person with one-quarter black ancestry.
- *Octoroon* referred to a person with one-eighth black ancestry.

These terms had legal significance in the South, since many people who had fair skin were legally slaves. In many cases, light-skinned slaves were chosen for domestic work inside the home, while darker-skinned slaves worked in the fields.

Today, these race classifications are considered offensive, and a growing number of Americans classify themselves as "mixed race"—nine million people, almost 3 percent of the population, in the 2010 census.

All their lives, Emily and her siblings had been taught by their mother to conduct themselves with dignity and modesty. Now, they had to stand before strangers and allow them to violate their privacy and touch them as they pleased—and they had to smile all the while or face the whip. She had been spared for the moment, but Emily knew that it was a matter of time before she and her sister would be chosen.

WITNESS TO HORRORS

Behind the closed doors of the showroom, beyond the view of the public, Emily witnessed the horrors and cruelty of the southern slave system. Not long after she arrived at the slave pen, Emily

The Second Wife

In New Orleans, attractive black women, both free and enslaved, were sometimes chosen as mistresses or second wives by wealthy French, Spanish, and Creole men. Through a social system known as *placage*, these men would take a woman of color as a secret common-law wife and separate their time between their two homes and families: one white, the other black; one public, the other private.

The women in these arrangements were not legally recognized as wives; they were known as *placées*, from the French word *placer*, meaning "to place with." Some women became *placées* voluntarily, if they were chosen by partners at so-called quadroon balls, formal dances where white men met fair-skinned women of color.

Many of these mixed-race families lived in neighborhoods not far from the slave pen where the Edmonsons were held.

"Creole women of color taking the air," an 1867 watercolor painting by Edouard Marquis. While these women would have been free in 1867, the *placage* system of "left-handed marriages" was well-established at the time the Edmonsons were in New Orleans.

met a young woman who was also from Alexandria, Virginia. The girl was quite small, and very fine looking, with beautiful long, straight hair. Emily didn't know her age, but she thought she was Mary's age, 15, or perhaps even younger. Shortly after they met, the girl was sold.

Emily didn't expect to see her again, but a few days later the girl returned. Emily overheard the overseer say that she had been returned because she did not suit her purchaser. The seller had to refund the dissatisfied buyer's money, and he was enraged at the girl for not being more cooperative. Emily did not watch the girl getting flogged, but she saw the brutal consequences. The girl had been whipped so viciously that sections of her flesh had been shredded into bloody strips. Emily was not surprised that the girl was beaten, but she did not understand why the slave owner would express his anger by destroying his property, or what was considered his property in the eyes of the law.

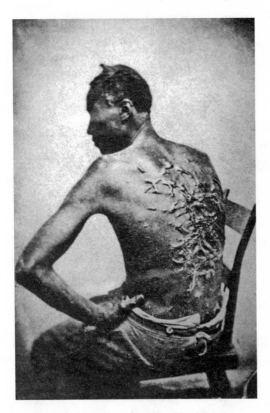

This iconic 1863 photograph shows the scars of a Mississippi slave who was beaten by his overseer.

Not long after the beating, Emily heard the overseer say that he would never flog another girl in that way again because, he said, it was too much for anyone to bear. Emily wondered if the guard experienced this change of heart because he observed his victim's ongoing suffering during weeks of painful recovery; it is one thing to snap a whip and another to witness the gore.

The cruelty never seemed to end. Not long after the incident with the Alexandria girl, a young man was also returned to the slave trader. The man who bought him claimed that he was not a good worker; the enslaved man said that he was brokenhearted because he and the woman he loved had been sold to different owners and separated. The slave owner refunded the buyer's money and then pledged to flog the slave nightly for a week.

Each stroke of the slave trader's bullwhip cut a bloody gash across the man's back. After about 200 lashes, the slave trader tired. He then demanded that each of the male slaves in the prison lay on five additional lashes with all his strength. Anyone who did not whip his fellow slave harshly enough was subjected to being flogged himself.

THE LASH.

This 1863 lithograph by Henry Louis Stephens depicts a slave being whipped. Beatings often ranged from 10 to 40 lashes, sometimes more. A pregnant woman would be forced to lie facedown with her abdomen in a pit so that she could be whipped without injury to the baby.

In the slave yard, beatings were not limited to adults. No one confined there—male or female, young or old—was allowed to sleep in the daytime. Sometimes young children would become drowsy and take a brief nap in the afternoon; if the overseer caught the children asleep, they were beaten. Emily and Mary would watch the little ones and let them doze off for brief periods of time, rousing them when they heard the keepers approach.

While most punishments were not designed to kill, in the New Orleans pen, the girls learned of two people—a woman and a young boy—who were whipped to death. Emily did not know how she was going to survive the ongoing abuse. In times of despair, other slaves found themselves almost envying those who had died: In death, they had at last found freedom; their suffering had ended.

⪟ TEN ⪞

An Unexpected Reunion

ICHARD EDMONSON ARRIVED in New Orleans a free
man. He had to wait for weeks for his return voyage
to Baltimore, so he decided to try to locate his older
brother, Hamilton, the oldest of the 14 Edmonson children.
Hamilton had run away from his owner's house in Washington,
D.C., on July 1, 1833. The only information Richard had was that
his brother had been captured and sold at auction in New Orleans,
destined to work in the cotton fields. Sixteen years had passed;
Richard had no reason to believe he would ever find out what
happened to Hamilton.

Richard interviewed every willing black person he encountered.
He went from shop to shop, asking for information about a slave
meeting Hamilton's description coming from Washington 16 years
before. After several days of searching, Richard wandered into a
cooper shop at 121 Girard Street in New Orleans. Although they
had grown up together, Richard did not recognize the store owner at
first. After several questions, however, it became clear that Richard
had found his oldest brother.

As they became reacquainted, Hamilton told Richard of his
experiences as a southern slave. After spending years on a cotton

plantation, Hamilton was sold again and given the last name of his new owner, Taylor. Hamilton Taylor became a cooper, a skilled tradesman who made barrels. While not a common practice, Hamilton's owner allowed him to keep a portion of his wages to encourage loyalty and to reduce the risk that he would run away. In time, Hamilton had saved enough money to buy his freedom for $1,000. As a free man, Hamilton started his own business making barrels near the shipping yard.

After 16 years away, Hamilton was eager to see the other members of his family. Mary had been a baby when Hamilton last saw her and Emily had not been born. Richard told Hamilton about his other siblings: Their five older sisters—Elizabeth, Eveline, Martha, Henrietta, and Eliza—were free, having purchased their freedom or married men who secured their freedom before the weddings. Their owner refused to sell any of the others because he depended on the steady income he received from hiring them out. The six who ran away on the *Pearl*—Emily, Mary, and their four brothers—had worked as domestic slaves before escaping. The two youngest, Josiah and Louisa, remained at home with their parents because they were still too young to be hired out. When he left the Culvers', Hamilton never expected to see his family again; now somehow Richard had found him. They had been given a second chance at brotherhood.

SURVIVING NEW ORLEANS

Emily did not know him and Mary did not remember him, but it did not take long for Hamilton to become a trusted member of the Edmonson family. The girls had heard stories about him, but they never expected to meet their runaway brother; finding Hamilton was their one experience of joy since they had arrived in New Orleans. Hamilton had not only survived, but thrived, even in the South.

   Hamilton tried to do all he could to help his brothers and sisters. At the New Orleans slave pen, Emily and Mary slept on the floor in the female section with about 20 or 30 other women. Mosquitoes and other insects swarmed the room at night, and every morning the girls woke to find their feet itchy and swollen with bug bites. Hamilton and Richard approached the slave trader and asked him for permission to have Emily and Mary sleep at Hamilton's house, with the understanding that they would return to the showroom each morning. The trader wanted his slaves to look as healthy and free of disease as possible, so he agreed to the arrangement, knowing that the promise of a life-threatening beating would be enough to prevent the girls from trying to run away.

   On the first night in Hamilton's home, Emily lay down on a mattress free of bugs and woke feeling more rested than she had in weeks. True to their word, she and Mary promptly returned to the slave pen to present themselves for sale.

   Not long after, Emily's confidence was shaken when she saw the overseer take Samuel away in a carriage. They had no chance to speak or say good-bye. When they learned that he had been sold, they were not allowed to weep or appear sad; they needed to appear joyful and industrious on display. Emily did not know if she would ever see Samuel again, but the following day he returned to the slave pen and told the girls that he had been sold as a butler to Horace Cammack, a wealthy cotton merchant who had paid $1,000 for him. Hamilton may have helped him secure the position, but the details aren't known. Relieved that Samuel had avoided the harshness of field work, Emily found peace in knowing that he had found what he thought would be the best possible arrangement under the circumstances. The similar sale of Ephraim and John, the two other enslaved Edmonson brothers in New Orleans, followed.

While Emily waited to be sold, she noticed that many of the enslaved people in the showroom fell ill, complaining of fever, nausea, and headache. Some bled from their mouths or vomited a substance that looked like blackened tar. As the days wore on, a growing number of those around her turned a ghastly shade of yellow, a sign of liver failure and the final stages of the disease known as yellow fever.

Every day more people succumbed to illness. Surrounded by death, the Edmonsons did not know how long they would be spared. They were not used to the weather and conditions in the South, and purchasers often hesitated to pay full price for slaves who might come down with "yellow jack." Would they fall victim to disease before they had a chance to experience freedom?

Just as abruptly as they had been sent to New Orleans, Emily, Mary, and Richard were ordered to go back to Virginia before they became sick. On July 6, after three weeks in the South, they boarded the *Union* for the second time. Emily may have hesitated to return to the ship, but she longed for home more than she feared seasickness. The slave trader had told Emily and Mary that their family had raised a significant amount of money on their behalf. Richard was returning to life as a free man and the girls hoped that when they arrived, freedom papers would be waiting for them, too.

Beware! Yellow Fever

Yellow fever was a serious health problem in 1848. The year before, the disease had claimed almost 3,000 lives in New Orleans. When the disease began to spread among the slaves, no one had any idea how many would die. To minimize the risk of losing valuable property, traders often moved their slaves out of the area when disease broke out.

At the time, no one understood that yellow fever is a virus spread by the bite of an infected mosquito. Three to six days after being bitten, a person would experience headache, muscle aches, fever, flushing, loss of appetite, vomiting, and jaundice (yellow skin and eyes). After three or four days, these symptoms would disappear; some people would recover at this point, and others relapsed after about 24 hours. If the disease progressed, an infected person experienced organ failure, seizures, coma, and death. In 1848, there was no prevention or cure for yellow fever. Today there is a vaccination for the disease and there are modern treatments for the symptoms.

The mosquito known as *Stegomyia aegypti* is responsible for spreading yellow fever.

❦ ELEVEN ❦

$2,250: The Price of Freedom

A S SOON AS Emily boarded the *Union*, she realized that the return trip to Baltimore wasn't going to be much easier than the trip to New Orleans had been. The belowdecks cargo area that had been crowded with slaves during their journey south was now packed to the ceiling with bales of cotton, barrels of molasses, and loaves of sugar. Emily and Mary were left with a space about eight or ten square feet directly under the hatchway door. To keep from getting seasick, Emily decided to avoid the confined cargo space, instead spending as much time as possible on deck in the fresh air. To make them more comfortable during the trip, Richard had been able to acquire and bring along a mattress, blankets, and extra food and drink.

After 16 days at sea, they arrived in Baltimore. The slave trader took Emily and Mary back to the same pen where they had been held the month before. Emily anticipated good news of her release when she met Jacob Bigelow, a Washington lawyer, who arrived a few hours later. He told Emily and Mary that he came to make sure that Richard was not delayed or harassed on his trip home to his wife and children, but, he explained, they were to remain. Not enough money had been raised to pay for their release.

Devastated, Emily realized that this time she and Mary would have to manage without the support and protection of their brothers.

Over the next few weeks, Emily and Mary fell into a predictable routine. In the mornings they were forced to exercise by marching around the yard to the music of fiddles and banjos; in the afternoons they washed and ironed, slept some, and often wept.

A few weeks later, Emily had a chance to see her father, Paul Edmonson, and her older sister, Elizabeth Brent, when they traveled to Baltimore to try to negotiate for the girls' release. The slave trader told Paul that he had two weeks to raise the funds or the girls would be moved to another slave market.

That night Elizabeth stayed with Emily and Mary in the women's area and Paul slept in the room above his daughters. Emily could hear her father crying and groaning through the night. In the morning, Paul stood in the yard of the slave pen and watched the slaves marching around. The yard was narrow and the girls walked past him, so close that their skirts almost brushed up against him, but they had to keep walking and he had to let them go. Overwhelmed with grief, Paul could not stop from crying out, "Oh, my children, my children!" Emily knew that her father feared that he would not have enough time to raise the necessary funds to buy his children's freedom.

BACK TO BRUIN & HILL

Weeks passed and Paul Edmonson did not return. Instead, Joseph Bruin, the slave trader from Alexandria, came to reclaim Emily and Mary. He roused the girls from their cell at about eleven o'clock at night and told them to come with him because they were returning to Virginia.

This time, Emily did not dare to consider the possibility of freedom. Surely, if she and Mary were to be free, Bruin would tell them. He said nothing.

At about 2 a.m., they arrived at Bruin & Hill in Alexandria, Virginia, the first place they were taken after leaving the Washington City Jail. They were placed in the same room where they had been held after their initial capture. Weeks had passed and they were back where they started.

Emily and Mary spent the sweltering days of August in the Alexandria slave pen washing, ironing, and sewing. Sometimes they were allowed to work in Bruin's house, located less than a block from the slave pen. They spent a lot of time looking after Bruin's children, seven-year-old Mary and four-year-old Martha, who developed a special affection for their caregivers.

COMING TO TERMS

Several weeks later, Paul Edmonson visited Bruin in Alexandria, trying once more to negotiate for his daughters' freedom. He planned to go north to raise funds but he wanted Bruin to state in writing the exact terms that he would accept for their release.

In response, Bruin drafted the following document:

Alexandria, Va., Sept. 5, 1848

The bearer, Paul Edmondson, is the father of two girls, Mary Jane and Emily Catherine Edmondson. These girls have been purchased by us, and once sent to the south; and upon the positive assurance that the money for them would be raised if they were brought back, they were returned. Nothing, it appears, has as yet been done in this respect by those who promised, and we are on the very eve of sending them south the second time; and we are candid in saying that if they go again, we will not regard any promises made in relation to them. The father wishes to raise money to pay for them; and intends to appeal to the liberality of the humane and the good to aid him, and has requested us to state in writing the conditions upon which we will sell his daughters.

We expect to start our service to the South in a few days; if the sum of twelve hundred ($1,200) dollars be raised and paid to us in fifteen days, or we be assured of that sum then we will retain them for twenty-five days more, to give an opportunity for the raising of the other thousand and fifty ($1,050) dollars; otherwise we shall be compelled to send them along with our other servants.

Bruin & Hill.

Paul Edmonson took the paper and left.

THE COFFLE DEPARTS

Emily and Mary waited anxiously for a letter or message from their father, but day after day passed without word from him. The letter stated that their father had 15 days, until September 20, to raise the ransom. Emily watched as the deadline approached—and then passed. Had the price been set so high that he would be unable to raise the money? Since Bruin had not received any payment, Emily realized that he was free to sell them any time he wished.

Just as Bruin had promised, he began preparations to send about 35 slaves in a coffle to South Carolina. Emily and Mary would be part of that chain gang.

The girls were given bright calico fabric and ordered to sew the show dresses that they would wear when they arrived and were exhibited for sale. Emily did as she was told, although all the time she spent cutting and stitching the fabric she felt as if she were sewing her own funeral shroud. Would she and Mary have to endure the same horrors and humiliations they had experienced in New Orleans?

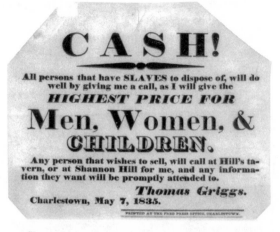

CASH!

All persons that have SLAVES to dispose of, will do well by giving me a call, as I will give the

HIGHEST PRICE FOR

Men, Women, & CHILDREN.

Any person that wishes to sell, will call at Hill's tavern, or at Shannon Hill for me, and any information they want will be promptly attended to.

Thomas Griggs.

Charlestown, May 7, 1835.

PRINTED AT THE FREE PRESS OFFICE, CHARLESTOWN.

Slave traders advertised in newspapers and broadsides for the purchase of slaves.

The night before the coffle was to leave, Emily and Mary went to Bruin's house to tell his family good-bye. His young daughters clung to Emily and Mary and begged them not to go. Mary explained that they did not want to leave, but they had to obey her father. Emily told Bruin's daughters that if they wanted them to stay, they should go and talk to their father. The children ran away to beg their father to allow Emily and Mary to remain in Virginia.

That night, Emily and Mary wept in the darkness of their cell. Bruin heard their cries and came up to see them. Mary begged for compassion, urging him to think of his own dear daughters. Bruin listened to Mary's words and hesitatingly agreed that if his business partner, Captain Henry Hill, approved, he would not force them to join the coffle leaving in the morning. That said, he warned the girls not to expect special treatment, since Hill had already said that he thought the girls should have been sold long ago.

Emily and Mary continued to weep and pray through the night. Morning dawned, but they had not been told that they could stay. Had Hill ignored their pleas? They gathered their few possessions and put on their bonnets and shawls. Had all their prayers gone unanswered?

Emily knew that in just a few moments, they would be forced to gather in the yard and line up—men, women, and children, two and two, the men handcuffed together, the right wrist of one to the left wrist of the other. A chain would be passed through the handcuffs, one after the other, linking the group together. The prisoners would form a line and travel on foot; the traders would travel on horseback on either side of the line, carrying whips to control both the horses and the people. At the time of their departure, they would be forced to set off singing—singing!—accompanied by fiddles and banjos, the steady crash of the chains creating the rhythm of the march.

A Slave-Coffle passing the Capitol.

From the 1881 book, *A Popular History of the United States*, by William Cullen Bryant. The men were typically handcuffed and chained together, while the women and children marched behind. The etching shows the U.S. Capitol as it appeared in 1815, without a dome.

Would they be able to survive the journey? Death was not unexpected when traveling on a chain gang.

Emily looked out the upstairs window of their quarters, watching the slaves gather in the yard below. When would she and Mary be called to join them?

The enslaved took their places in line, shackled together.

The fiddle and banjo began to play.

The gates to the pen opened and the coffle began to shuffle forward.

Sorrow Songs

Coffles were often led by fiddle and banjo players to keep the enslaved marching at a steady pace and to conceal their sorrow. Frederick Douglass reflected on the meaning of music and song among slaves in his 1845 book, *Narrative of the Life of Frederick Douglass, An American Slave*:

> I have often been utterly astonished, since I came to the north, to find persons who could speak of the singing among slaves as evidence of their contentment and happiness. It is impossible to conceive of a greater mistake. . . . The songs of the slave represent the sorrow of his heart; and he is relieved by them, only as an aching heart is relieved by its tears.

Frederick Douglass (1818–1895), a reformer and leader in the abolitionist movement, understood the extreme hardships of living within slavery. He was born Frederick Augustus Washington Bailey and changed his name to Douglass after escaping to the North.

Emily and Mary watched them leave, watched the last person in line move out of the yard and the gates close behind him. They had been spared. When they understood they would *not* be going to South Carolina, they hugged each other and wept with relief. They were not free, but they did not have to go south, not yet, not that day.

What Emily and Mary did not know was that the night before the coffle departed, Joseph Bruin met with one of the Edmonsons' supporters, probably William Chaplin, and worked out a last-minute agreement to keep the girls in Virginia. The man offered Bruin a $600 deposit, which he could keep if Paul Edmonson failed to come up with the balance of the money due by a new deadline.

Bruin, eager to pocket the $600 bonus, agreed to the arrangement. He no longer expected the Edmonsons to be able to raise the money. After all, they had been trying for months without success. Why would things be different this time?

TWELVE

Ransomed

PAUL EDMONSON ASKED everyone he knew for help raising the money he needed to buy his daughters' freedom, but he had only limited success. When he approached abolitionist sympathizers in Washington, they didn't have money to offer, but they did make arrangements for him to go to New York City to ask for assistance from the American and Foreign Anti-Slavery Society. After a 12-hour train ride, Paul arrived in Manhattan and followed the directions he had been given to the main office of the society. He explained his situation and shared testimonials about the girls' good character as well as a letter from Rev. Mathew Turner, the white minister at Asbury Methodist Church where the Edmonsons had worshiped, which stated that they were exemplary members of the congregation and worthy of support. A representative from the Anti-Slavery Society agreed to follow up by writing to Bruin to authenticate the facts of the case and to see if he would lower the ransom.

In the meantime, Paul was directed to the Rev. James W. C. Pennington, an escaped slave from Maryland who was also a founding member of the American Anti-Slavery Society and pastor of

The American Anti-Slavery Society

T he American Anti-Slavery Society was founded in 1833 and dedicated to ending slavery in the United States. Within five years, it had
about 1,500 state and local chapters and more than 200,000 members.

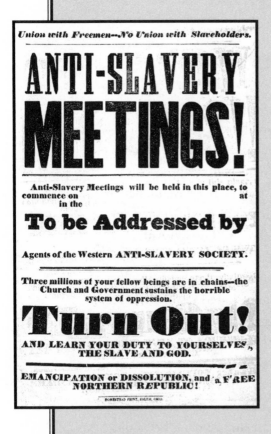

Slavery was a divisive moral and eco-
nomic issue, and pro-slavery mobs
sometimes disrupted meetings and
attacked speakers.

Even within the society, members did not agree on how to achieve
their goals. The more radical members of the group denounced the
U.S. Constitution as pro-slavery and
favored allowing women to take
leadership roles within the group.
The more conservative faction supported working for change within the
government, and it expected women
to leave the work of the organiza-
tion to the men. In 1839, a more
conservative group known as the
American and Foreign Anti-Slavery
Society splintered off. At the same
time, some members left and formed
a third group, the Liberty Party,
which aimed to end slavery through
the political process. Following this organizational change, most work in
the abolitionist movement was done through state and local branches or
chapters.

This woodcut image titled "Am I not a man and a brother?" was originally used as the seal of the Society for the Abolition of Slavery in England in the 1780s. It was widely used in the American abolitionist movement as well.

the Shiloh Presbyterian Church in New York City. Pennington preached about the Edmonson case in his church the following Sunday and his congregation raised $50 in donations, a significant amount of money considering that most members of the church were quite poor and many were saving their money to free their own family members. Paul didn't want to appear ungrateful—he did appreciate the efforts being made to help his family—but $50 wasn't nearly enough for him to reach his goal in time. Pennington understood and sent Paul to visit the home of the Rev. Henry Ward Beecher, a preacher and the editor of the New York *Independent*, an abolitionist newspaper.

When Paul arrived at Beecher's house in Brooklyn, no one was home, so he sat on the front steps to wait. Overcome with stress and grief, he could no longer hold back the tears and he began to weep. When Beecher arrived, Paul gathered his composure and explained his situation. Beecher invited him inside to his library to tell his story.

Before that time, Beecher had not taken up the cause of slavery from the pulpit, but Mary and Emily's story horrified him. The girls were so young and innocent that he felt compelled to act. Beecher, who had led the Plymouth Church in Brooklyn for about a year, reached out to other churches and congregations, inviting them to attend a public rally to benefit the girls. This ecumenical appeal was the first time New York clergy from different denominations had come together to assist slaves in need.

GATHERING AT THE TABERNACLE

On the night of October 23, 1848, 2,000 people from across New York City jammed into the Broadway Tabernacle at Worth and Catherine streets. Paul watched Beecher captivate the audience with his zeal and theatrics. Early in his remarks, Beecher held up shackles and chains and dramatically clashed them onto a table in front of him.

Paul admired the way Beecher carefully chose his words. Rather than wrestling with broad questions about the system of slavery itself, Beecher focused on the plight of Emily and Mary Edmonson, two devout and virginal Christian girls who faced a life of prostitution in the South if he and his congregation failed to act.

Rev. Henry Ward Beecher: Finding His Voice

Henry Ward Beecher was born in Litchfield, Connecticut, in 1813. He was a shy and sensitive child with a severe speech impediment. "When Henry is sent to me with a message, I always have to make him say it three times," said one of his aunts.

Beecher took oratorical training at Mount Pleasant Classical Institute, a boarding school in Amherst, Massachusetts, before studying at Amherst College and later at Lane Theological Seminary outside Cincinnati, Ohio. In his own words:

Henry Ward Beecher was one of the best-known clergymen of the day. Several of his brothers and sisters became respected educators and abolitionists, including his sister Harriet Beecher Stowe.

> I had from childhood a thickness of speech arising from a large palate, so that when a boy I used to be laughed at for talking as if I had pudding in my mouth. When I went to Amherst, I was fortunate in passing into the hands of John Lovell, a teacher of elocution; and a better teacher for my purpose I cannot conceive. His system consisted in drill, or the thorough practice of inflexions by the voice, of gesture, posture, and articulation. Sometimes I was a whole hour practicing my voice on a word, like justice.
>
> I would have to take a posture, frequently a mark chalked on the floor. Then we would go through all the gestures; exercising each movement of the arm, and the throwing open the hand. . . . It was drill, drill, drill, until the motions almost became second nature. Now I never know what movement I shall make. My gestures are natural because this drill made them natural to me.

Beecher overcame his speech problems, and his antislavery preaching then made him one of the most prominent orators of his time.

While sympathetic to the Edmonsons as individuals, not everyone believed that ransom should be paid for slaves. Some people thought that negotiating with slaveholders recognized and legitimized the institution of slavery. Others believed that paying ransom would just supply money to those who would use it to buy other slaves. In addition, some didn't consider it fair to use limited resources to ransom the fortunate few rather than promote the emancipation of all enslaved people.

Despite these objections, most audience members found Beecher's plea hard to resist because it focused on the fate of two specific individuals. It wasn't abstract, it was personal. The audience at the Broadway Tabernacle wasn't trying to take on the institution of slavery; it was trying to help two innocent Christian girls, Emily and Mary Edmonson.

Beecher presented Paul to the audience and asked: "The father! Do goods and chattel have fathers? Do slaves have daughters?" He spoke of the girls' spirituality and faithfulness, begging the audience to protect the virtue of these Christian girls. When he noted that they were pious members of the Episcopal

The Broadway Tabernacle was a center of antislavery activism from its founding in 1836. A pro-slavery mob burned it down while it was under construction, but it was rebuilt.

PLYMOUTH CHURCH. REV. HENRY WARD BEECHER SELLING A SLAVE.

Methodist Church and that their faith would make them worth more on the slave market, the crowd responded with fury.

Paul watched as a fire was lit within Beecher. The chains before him became a symbol of the chains that bound Emily and Mary, as well as those that held the wrists of millions of other slaves, and in an outburst of passion Beecher seized them, slammed them to the floor, and ground them beneath his heel as though he were grinding the institution of slavery to dust beneath his feet. The audience cheered; their applause thundered throughout the hall.

"I thank you for that noise!" Beecher said. "It cheers me and makes me feel that I am among brethren." Beecher paced the stage—talking, preaching, waving his hands. A man in the audience later described him as "popping about like a box of fireworks

Rev. Henry Ward Beecher held mock auctions to raise funds to ransom enslaved persons, including Emily and Mary Edmonson.

Was It Wrong to Ransom Mary and Emily?

Many abolitionists were reluctant to pay to ransom slaves, even though they wanted to end slavery. They had several key concerns:

- Negotiating with slaveholders recognized and legitimized the institution of slavery. If abolitionists didn't believe one person had the right to own another, how could they engage in this kind of commerce?
- Paying ransom provided money to those who could use it to buy additional slaves. Wouldn't buying slaves drive up the prices and give slave traders the money they needed to stay in business?
- Using money to ransom individual slaves misused funds that could otherwise be used to promote the emancipation of all enslaved people. Should the resources of the abolitionists be used to free all slaves, not just the fortunate few?
- Engaging in the buying and selling of human beings was sinful and morally wrong. Was it ever appropriate to do what is wrong, even if the goal was to achieve a greater good?

accidentally ignited and going off in all shapes and directions—a rocket here with falling stars, a fiery wheel there."

Beecher then called for a donation, urging the audience to be generous.

When the money was counted, it amounted to a mere $600. Edmonson needed $2,250. Beecher expressed his displeasure and a voice came from the crowd: "Take up another!"

The collection boxes circulated again. This time members of the audience dug deeper into their pockets. Some women in the audience removed their rings and earrings and added their valuable jewelry to the collection. The money was counted, and again it fell several hundred dollars short.

One by one, additional pledges were made. Mr. S. B. Chittenden gave his name for another $50; his brother, Henry Chittenden, matched the pledge with $50 more. From time to time a voice in the audience yelled, "How much is wanting now?"

When all but $50 had been raised, Beecher said, "I never did hurrah in a public meeting, but when this account is closed up, I will join in three of the loudest cheers that ever rang through this old building."

"I'll take the balance," called a member of Beecher's Plymouth Church.

The room erupted in cheers and shouts. Men waved their hats and handkerchiefs offering three cheers for Beecher and the benefactors.

Paul broke down in tears.

After a moment of revelry, Beecher quieted the crowd and reminded them of the gratitude they each owed to God. Those in attendance sang the doxology, "Praise God from whom all blessings flow," not with thunder and applause, but with tenderness and thanksgiving.

The meeting closed with a joyful benediction, celebrating the fact that the Edmonson sisters would soon be free.

PAYMENT IN FULL

On an afternoon in early November, Emily was sewing near the open window of Bruin's home when she looked outside and said: "There, Mary, is that white man we have seen from the North." A moment later and they noticed a second man—their father!—walking with the man.

They sprang up and ran through the house and into the street, shouting as they went. The girls knew their father had been collecting money in the North. Emily rushed to him and asked if he had been successful. Paul's hands shook and his voice trembled as he told his daughters that he needed to speak with Bruin but would talk to them soon. Paul Edmonson and his companion entered Bruin's office and shut the door.

Emily and Mary returned to their room while their father conducted his business with Bruin. Did their father have the money for their ransom?

Did he have enough for both of them?

The longer they waited, the more they worried. They focused on their father's trembling hands and unsteady voice. Could he, in fact, be bringing them bad news? They had heard that their mother had been quite ill. Was she dead or in failing health? They strode back and forth as anxiety turned to excitement and back into anxiety again.

➜ ←

Inside the office, Bruin said that he was sincerely glad that Paul had arrived with the payment and that he would honor their agreement, but he was disappointed that Beecher had spoken so harshly about him at the meeting at the tabernacle. Bruin considered himself a good Christian and a more humane and sophisticated man than other slave traders. (Most slave traders were wealthy and influential citizens from well-to-do plantation families.) Bruin may have been well dressed and had impeccable manners, but he still made his fortune buying and selling human beings. Business was business.

Bruin counted the money, $2,250 cash, and signed the bill of sale. It read:

> Received from W. L. Chaplin twenty-two hundred and fifty dollars, being payment in full for the purchase of two negroes, named Mary and Emily Edmonson. The right and title of said negroes we warrant and defend against the claims of all persons whatsoever; and likewise warrant them sound and healthy in body and mind, and slaves for life.

Given under our hand and seal, this seventh day of November, 1848. $2,250 BRUIN & Hill. (Seal.)

Bruin handed the paper to William Chaplin, who had helped plan the escape on the *Pearl*. When Bruin let go, Mary and Emily Edmonson were no longer his.

FOREVER FREE

Upstairs, Emily paced and prayed and tried to stay calm. She tried to accept Mary's reassurance that God's will would be done, whether she and Mary would be freed or if they would suffer another setback.

Finally, a messenger came shouting to them, "You are free! You are free!"

The girls jumped and clapped and laughed and shouted.

Paul held his daughters tenderly and tried to quiet them. He certainly shared their exuberance, but he may have known that even as free women their lives would not be free of hardship and discrimination. He told them to prepare to go home and see their mother. The girls gathered their belongings and said good-bye to members of the Bruin family, this time with joy rather than sadness.

A carriage took the girls and their father to their sister Elizabeth's house in Washington, where family and friends had gathered to celebrate their emancipation. Their brothers lifted the girls in their arms and ran about with them, almost frantic with joy. Their mother wept and gave thanks to God. They spent the night rejoicing, grateful for the chance to be together.

In the morning, Mary and Emily went with Chaplin to City Hall and watched him sign the deed of manumission. In exchange for a payment of one dollar, the document assured that "the sisters Mary Jane and Emily Catherine Edmonson, daughters of Paul Edmonson," were "hereby, each of them, declared forever free from any and all restraint or control." After a lifetime of slavery and more than six months in various slave pens and auction houses, Mary and Emily belonged only to themselves. They were, at last, free.

THIRTEEN

The Trial of Captain Daniel Drayton

W HILE EMILY AND Mary were ransomed about seven months after they first tried to escape, the captains of the *Pearl* remained in prison. Although there were two captains aboard the ship on the night of the escape, the central figure in the plot was 46-year-old Captain Daniel Drayton.

After the passengers and crew of the *Pearl* were captured, Drayton was questioned about the events of that night. Those who interrogated him wanted to know who had masterminded and financed the escape, but Drayton refused to tell them. He knew that to reveal the names of his contacts in New York and Philadelphia would not only put his associates at personal risk but could also compromise the broader abolitionist movement.

The names he kept secret were William L. Chaplin's, of the New York Anti-Slavery Society, and Dr. Charles Cleveland's, of the Philadelphia Anti-Slavery Society. These two men had raised the money and organized the escape plan, arranging for Drayton to be paid $100 to smuggle a group of enslaved people out of Washington, D.C. Drayton was given another $100 to hire a boat and captain.

Most of the seamen Drayton approached refused to help him with a scheme as risky as a slave escape. Captain Edward Sayres needed work and the $100 fee was significantly more than he could earn in another trip of similar duration. The men agreed that Drayton would control the cargo—the enslaved people—and Sayres would control the ship itself.

Drayton did not tell his captors anything, and he was sent back to his cell. When it came time to sleep, one of the keepers threw Drayton two thin blankets and left him to rest as well as he could on the stone floor. The room was virtually empty—no chair, table, stool, just a night bucket and a water can.

A WELCOME VISITOR

In the morning, Ohio Congressman Joshua Giddings and his friend Edwin Hamlin, editor of the Cleveland daily *True Democrat*, an antislavery newspaper, arrived at the jail to visit Drayton and Sayres. As they entered the building, they had to work their way through a cluster of slave owners and slave traders doing business in the lobby. When 53-year-old Giddings asked to visit the prisoners, the jailer hesitated. He knew who was standing before him; Giddings, who believed that slavery violated not just the Constitution but a higher natural law, was known as one of the most outspoken antislavery legislators of his day. He wasn't sure it would be safe to let a well-known abolitionist and a newspaper editor inside the jail to visit the accused.

Eventually the jailer allowed them in, relocking the front gate and passing the key back to another guard. He then escorted the men up the winding stone staircase to a second locked gate, which he opened to allow Giddings and Hamlin to pass through to the cells where Drayton and Sayres were held.

When the congressman met Drayton, he reassured the captain that his friends in the abolitionist movement would not
abandon him. In that moment, Drayton had the power to derail
several leading members of the Underground Railroad by linking
them to criminal activity. Giddings reiterated that he and his abolitionist associates would take care of Drayton's family if he stayed
quiet and did not provide the names of those who had planned
the escape. In addition to financial support, Giddings offered
Drayton representation by an attorney, David A. Hall, a lawyer
from the District of Columbia who had experience defending
several people who had been implicated in another Underground
Railroad escape.

While Giddings spoke with Drayton, the noise of the rioters
echoed in the staircase. Not long after, their voices grew louder
and Giddings could hear dozens of feet pounding up the stairs.
Downstairs, someone in the mob had gained possession of the
key and unlocked the first gate, allowing the men to rush up the
stairs and continue to threaten and yell at the congressman, who
had become the target for their anger.

Although they were still separated by a second locked iron
gate, someone in the crowd told Giddings to leave immediately
or his life would be in danger. Giddings ignored the threats and
completed his business with Drayton. He refused to show fear or
any willingness to retreat.

The jailer eventually regained control of the crowd and convinced the men on the stairs to move back behind the main gate
so that the visitors could leave. Giddings calmly faced the mob,
meeting the eyes of those who had come to do him harm. The
protesters had felt bold enough to assault the congressman with
words, but no one touched him as he passed. Giddings and Hamlin walked down the stairs and out the front door unharmed.

Addressing Congress About the *Pearl* Escape

After visiting Captain Daniel Drayton in the Washington City Jail, Congressman Joshua Giddings went to the floor of the House of Representatives to speak about the escape on the *Pearl*. The following is an excerpt of his April 25, 1848, speech:

It is said that some seventy-six men, women, and children, living in this District, possessing the same natural right to the enjoyment of life and liberty as gentlemen in this Hall . . . went on board a schooner lying at one of the wharves of this city, and set sail for a "land of liberty."

When they reached the mouth of the river, adverse winds compelled them to anchor. Thus detained, we may imagine the anxiety that must have filled their minds. How that slave mother pressed her tender babe more closely to her breast, as she sent up to the God of the oppressed her silent supplication for deliverance from the men-stealers who were on their track. . . . Bloodhounds in human shape were in her pursuit, clothed with the authority of the laws enacted by Congress, and now kept in force by this body. They seized upon those wretched fugitives and brought them back to this city, and thrust them into yonder prison, erected by the treasure of this nation.

There they remained until Friday, when nearly fifty of them, having been purchased by the infamous [slave trader] Hope H. Slatter, who headed the mob at the jail on Tuesday, were taken . . . to the railroad depot, and from thence to Baltimore, destined for sale in the far south, there to drag out a miserable existence upon the cotton and sugar plantations of that slave-consuming region.

The scene at the depot is represented as one which would have disgraced the city of Algiers or Tunis: Wives bidding adieu to their husbands, mothers in an agony of despair, unable to bid farewell to their daughters; little boys and girls weeping amid the general distress, scarcely knowing the cause of their grief. Sighs and groans and tears and unutterable agony, characterized a scene at which the heart sickens, and from which humanity shrinks with horror.

Over such a scene that fiend in human shape, Slatter, presided, assisted by some three or four associates in depravity, each armed with pistols, Bowie-knife, and club. Yes, sir, by virtue of our laws he held these mothers and children, these sisters and brothers, subject to his power, and tore them from the ties which bind mankind to life, and carried them south, and doomed them to cruel and lingering deaths.

Sir, do you believe that those members of this body, who stubbornly refused to repeal those laws, are less guilty in the sight of a just and holy God than Slatter himself? We, sir, enable him to pursue this accursed vocation. Can we be innocent of those crimes? How long will members of this House continue thus to outrage humanity?

Congressman Joshua R. Giddings (1795–1864) represented Ohio's 16th district. He was an outspoken opponent of slavery.

INDICTED

Later that day, a jailer escorted Drayton downstairs to an office where two justices of the peace, Hampton C. Williams and John H. Goddard, were prepared to hold court. They had decided to conduct official business inside the jail because they considered it too dangerous to move the accused over to the courthouse.

Before the proceedings began, United States District Attorney Philip Barton Key told Drayton's attorney that he should leave the jail and go home immediately, because the people outside were furious and he risked his life by representing Drayton. Unruffled, Hall replied that things had come to a pretty pass if a man no longer had the privilege of safely speaking with his counsel.

The grand jury, under the instructions of the district attorney, handed up 74 indictments against each of the prisoners. During the proceedings, the justices of the peace charged Drayton, Sayres, and Chester English with stealing and transporting slaves and fixed bail at $1,000 for each runaway aboard the *Pearl*, or $76,000 for each of the accused.

The district attorney wanted to find the men guilty of a penitentiary offense in addition to levying a fine, so he employed an arcane 1737 Maryland statute that provided that any person who steals a slave shall "suffer death as a felon and be excluded the benefit of clergy." A modification of the law in 1831 changed the punishment from death to confinement in a penitentiary for not less than 20 years.

→←

Neither Drayton nor Sayres could come up with the money needed to post bail, so they remained in the Washington City Jail to wait for their trials to begin. Drayton did his best to make prison life tolerable. Nothing could be done to improve the fact that his small stone cell had no direct sunlight and poor ventilation, but after about six weeks he was able to obtain an old mattress to place on the hard floor. A sympathetic cook sometimes gave him extra food on the side, but he found the basic prison food unappetizing. As a prisoner, Drayton received two meals a day: breakfast, consisting of one herring, corn bread, coffee, and a dish of molasses; and dinner, a second helping of corn bread, half a pound of salted beef, and a soup made of cornmeal. No fresh fruit or seasoned vegetables were served. In fact, the menu remained the same, day after day, month after month.

This portrait of Capt. Daniel Drayton was used to illustrate his 1853 book, *Personal Memoir of Daniel Drayton, for Four Years and Four Months a Prisoner (for Charity's Sake) in a Washington Jail.*

To make time pass faster, Drayton worked on self-improvement. When he first entered the jail, he could read reasonably well and he could sign his name, but he could not write in complete sentences. While he was incarcerated, he practiced writing and he read the newspaper whenever he could borrow a copy.

He also had time to think. Rather than weakening his resolve, Drayton's time in prison taught him to appreciate his freedom, and living without liberty strengthened his conviction that slavery was wrong.

THE TRIAL

Although the escape on the *Pearl* involved a single event, Drayton and Sayres were indicted on 110 separate charges: 36 larceny indictments for stealing from the 36 people who owned slaves on the *Pearl*, as well as the 74 grand jury indictments for transporting slaves. The charges against English were dropped in exchange for his testimony against the captains. If convicted on all counts, each of the men could have been sentenced to more than 800 years in prison. (The number of enslaved people reported to be involved in the case changed several times: 77 runaways boarded the *Pearl*, but bail was set based on 76 fugitives, and the grand jury handed down indictments for 74. The record does not explain the changing number, but it is possible that some enslaved people were later found to be free.)

The first trial against Drayton began on July 27, 1848. That day the temperature soared above 90 degrees and the high humidity made the air in the packed courtroom oppressive, even with the windows open for ventilation. The first case involved the escape of two enslaved men, Joe and Frank, who were the property of Andrew Hoover, the 47-year-old owner of a shoe factory and retail store. The district attorney argued that Drayton stole the men and intended to take them to the West Indies to sell them, although he did not explain why Drayton would have set off in an undersized boat that was not capable of sailing in the open ocean.

During the trial, Drayton's attorney attempted to call Joe and Frank as witnesses, but the judge ruled that the men did not have the right to testify in a District of Columbia court. Instead, the defense attorney called Hoover, who admitted under oath that no one had broken into his house; the property—the two enslaved men—had walked away on their own. If they left of their own volition, how could Drayton be found guilty of stealing them?

The case went to the jury at 3 p.m. When the court recon-
vened the following day at 10 a.m., the jury had not made a
decision. Four members of the jury hesitated to convict Drayton,
but the others eventually pressured the holdouts to change their
minds. After 24 hours of deliberation, the verdict was in: Drayton
was guilty.

Drayton wasn't surprised by the verdict, but he still wondered:
How could he be found guilty of stealing something that cannot
be owned? How can one man own another, any more than he can
own the sea or the sky or the stars?

One case followed another during legal maneuverings that
lasted almost one year. Ultimately, Sayres was cleared of all larceny charges and convicted of 74 counts of transporting slaves;
he was fined $7,400, or $100 for each conviction. Drayton was
convicted of two counts of larceny and 74 counts of transporting
slaves. The judge fined him $10,360, or $140 for each transporting conviction, a greater fine than Sayres's because he was deemed
more responsible for the crimes. Drayton was also sentenced to 20
years at hard labor for the larceny convictions. Both men were to
remain in jail until the fines were paid, which, as far as Drayton
was concerned, meant that they would be imprisoned for life.

In November 1848, Drayton appealed his larceny convictions
before a three-judge panel of the District of Columbia Circuit
Court. On February 19, 1849, judges William Cranch, James
Morsell, and James Dunlop struck down the decision, ruling
that for Drayton's larceny conviction to stand, he would have
had to profit from the escape. With these charges overturned,
the 20-year jail sentence was dropped, although he still had to
remain in prison until he could pay the outstanding fines.

❦ FOURTEEN ❧

A Radical Education

A FEW WEEKS AFTER Emily and Mary Edmonson were freed, Rev. Henry Beecher invited the young women to visit New York City so that they could personally thank their benefactors. He also planned a second rally on their behalf, hoping to raise money for their education. Emily and Mary accepted Beecher's invitation, excited to have a chance to thank those who had been so generous to them. On the trip, they were escorted by abolitionist William Chaplin, who had helped coordinate their release and took them to the ministers who had sponsored the first rally and contributed toward their ransom.

On the night of December 7, the hall at the Broadway Tabernacle was again filled with many of the same people who had helped raise the ransom for the girls weeks before. When the program started, the Rev. Samuel H. Cox, from the First Presbyterian Church in Brooklyn, took the podium and told the audience that he had been impressed with the gratitude and good manners shown by Emily and Mary, noting that he could not have expected better manners from the daughters of Queen Victoria of England.

Beecher took the podium and congratulated the crowd for having been so generous in the past. He introduced Emily and Mary, and the girls felt eyes—thousands of eyes—focusing on them, staring, pitying, judging, wondering what their suffering must have been like. Beecher held Emily and Mary's bill of sale over his head, waving it in the air, saying it was wrong to sell people as if they were animals.

As he spoke, Beecher's words became more radical and inflammatory. "Slavery is a state of suppressed war," he said. "The slave is justified in regarding his master as a belligerent enemy and in seizing him from whatever reprisals are necessary to aid him in effecting a retreat."

This is the only known photograph featuring the Edmonson sisters alone. Mary is standing with her hand on Emily's shoulder.

Emily had never heard such strong words about slavery before—certainly never from a preacher, never from the pulpit. Were his words true? Did enslaved people have the power to resist authority and run away?

When the audience seemed enthusiastic and responsive, Beecher called for contributions to establish an education fund for Emily and Mary. He urged the crowd to help them prepare for a life of usefulness, noting that they wanted to become teachers so that they could educate other black Americans.

The plate was passed, but this time few contributed.

Now that they were free, Emily and Mary had begun to recognize new possibilities in their lives. They were both eager to learn to read and then to teach. Emily knew that she would not let this lack of financial support stop her; she would find a way to learn to read and write and complete her education. Beecher tried, but even he could not make an appeal for the sisters' education fund as exciting as the appeal to save them from the chains of slavery.

Beecher did not want to accept defeat. He called for a second meeting at the Broadway Tabernacle a week later, but that crowd proved no more supportive. Many abolitionists did not consider black people to be their social or intellectual equals, even though they did favor ending slavery.

BOARDING SCHOOL

Even after they were freed, Chaplin continued to support Emily and Mary. He believed that they put a sympathetic face on the abuses of slavery, and that citizens in the North would object to slavery if they knew the kind of people who were held in bondage. He covered their educational expenses and made arrangements for the girls to move to upstate New York to live and study in the homes of several leading abolitionists, including Gerrit Smith and William R. Smith. Little is known about their early education, except that the girls excelled in their studies. By the fall of 1849 they were ready to attend New York Central College, a school run by abolitionists in McGrawville, New York.

For a time, the girls also stayed in the Syracuse home of Jermain Loguen, a runaway slave from Tennessee. Though surviving records don't describe details of the time they spent with Loguen, he was known to be a bold and fearless conductor on the Underground Railroad, the network of secret routes and safe houses used by runaway slaves during their escape to northern free states or Canada. Conductors

Jermain Wesley Loguen (1813–1872) ran away from slavery at age 21. He eventually settled in Syracuse, New York, where he opened his house to slaves on the Underground Railroad. In 1859, he wrote his autobiography, *The Rev. J. W. Loguen, as a Slave and as a Freeman, a Narrative of Real Life.*

sheltered fugitives and guided them from station to station, typically at night. Loguen operated his station so openly that he sometimes advertised in the newspaper that he offered assistance to runaway slaves. During the time they spent with Loguen, Emily and Mary almost certainly helped shelter and support fugitive slaves on their way to freedom.

BECOMING ABOLITIONISTS

In Loguen's home, slavery wasn't only personal, it was political. He not only assisted individual runaways, he also dedicated himself to changing public policy. In addition to their academic work, Emily and Mary often attended antislavery rallies with Loguen and other abolitionists. They lived in a household that discussed current events and politics, so they became familiar with the proposed Fugitive Slave Act, as well as legislation pending in Congress in 1850 that involved the spread of slavery into the new territories and states in the west. The act would give slave owners and their agents almost unlimited power to travel north to track down and reclaim runaway slaves. The law would also subject those who assisted fugitive slaves to fines of up to $1,000 and six months of jail time.

While Emily and Mary were legally free in both the North and the South, they were distraught that their good friend Loguen and other runaway slaves would be in jeopardy if the Fugitive Slave Act passed. For decades, Loguen had lived in the North as a free man, raising his family and serving as a minister. Passage of the new Fugitive Slave Act would mean that he could be uprooted and enslaved, captured and returned to his owner in Tennessee. Anyone who helped protect him—including Mary and Emily—could be fined and imprisoned.

This lithograph, titled "Effects of the Fugitive Slave Law," includes two texts at the bottom. The first quotation comes from Deuteronomy: "Thou shalt not deliver unto the master his servant which has escaped from his master unto thee. He shall dwell with thee. Even among you in that place which he shall choose in one of thy gates where it liketh him best. Thou shalt not oppress him." The second quote is from the Declaration of Independence: "We hold that all men are created equal, that they are endowed by their Creator with certain unalienable rights, that among these are life, liberty and the pursuit of happiness." Antislavery activists sold prints like this one to raise funds to promote their cause. The artist, Theodore Kaufmann (1814–1896), was a German immigrant and dedicated abolitionist.

In the summer of 1850, Loguen planned to attend a convention in Cazenovia, New York, to protest the proposed act, and he invited Emily and Mary to join him. The girls accepted and were delighted to find out that their old friend and supporter Chaplin was planning to attend the convention as well. They had learned so much since they saw him last; what would he think of them now?

The Fugitive Slave Act
and the Compromise of 1850

By the middle of the 19th century, the slavery issue demanded Congressional action. Most northern congressmen wanted Texas, New Mexico, and the land in the Southwest claimed in the Mexican-American War to be free of slavery, and, of course, most southern legislators wanted to spread slavery into these new territories. After extensive debates and discussions, Congress reached a compromise, known, appropriately, as the Compromise of 1850. It held that:

- California, where the Gold Rush was in full force, would be a free state;

- Texas would give up its claim to New Mexico and other territorial land in exchange for debt relief;

- The other former Mexican lands, including the Utah and New Mexico Territories, would be divided between free and slave;

- The buying and selling of slaves would be prohibited in Washington, D.C., although slave-owning states would remain legal and slave traders could continue to do business across the river in Virginia;

- The Fugitive Slave Act would be enacted. This act gave slaveholders almost unlimited power to track down and capture runaway slaves in the northern free states. It required federal marshals and other law enforcement officers to assist in the return of runaway slaves based only on the word of the claimant. It also made it illegal to assist fugitive slaves, with a penalty of up to a $1,000 fine and six months in prison. Suspected slaves had no right to jury trial or to testify or present evidence on their own behalf.

The Compromise consisted of five separate bills, all of which were passed in September 1850.

∾ FIFTEEN ∾

Chaplin's Surrender

A FEW WEEKS BEFORE the Cazenovia Convention, William Chaplin was in Washington, D.C., working with other abolitionists to defeat the Fugitive Slave Act. As part of a flamboyant plot designed to draw attention to the cause, Chaplin planned to arrive in Cazenovia with two runaway slaves hidden in his private two-horse carriage. To make the ploy even more worthy of news coverage, the slaves he planned to smuggle north belonged to Congressmen Robert Toombs and Alexander H. Stephens, both of Georgia.

On the appointed night, Chaplin drove his carriage down Seventh Street and out of Washington with the two fugitives, Allen and Garland, hidden in the back of his carriage. Although the specifics are unknown, someone alerted John Goddard of Washington's auxiliary guard to the plan. Goddard and six other men (four police officers and two civilian slave catchers) were waiting to ambush Chaplin and the runaways on their way out of town. As Chaplin crossed the Maryland state line, Goddard and his men leaped from the shadows and thrust a heavy wooden rail into one of the carriage wheels to stop it.

The carriage crashed to a halt. Rather than surrender peacefully, Chaplin and the runaways drew their pistols and shot at the officers,

William Chaplin (1796–1871) worked with the American Anti-Slavery Society and the Society for the State of New York.

who returned fire. During a five- or six-minute shootout, 27 bullets were fired, but astonishingly, no one was killed. One of the enslaved men was shot in the hand but still managed to run; the other survived the gun battle only because he had been carrying a large pocket watch that deflected a bullet that otherwise would have injured him.

After some hand-to-hand fighting, Chaplin was eventually taken into custody and arrested, and the fugitives were returned to their owners. Rather than making a heroic entrance at the convention, as he had planned, Chaplin joined the captains of the *Pearl* in the Washington City Jail.

THE CAZENOVIA CONVENTION

On August 21, 1850, Emily, Mary, and about 400 other people crowded into the Free Congregational Church in Cazenovia, New York, for the opening of the Cazenovia Fugitive Slave Law Convention. Hundreds of others gathered outside the building, unable to find a seat in the pews. Frederick Douglass, already famous for his 1845 autobiography, *Narrative of the Life of Frederick Douglass, An American Slave*, presided over the meeting and told the audience about Chaplin's arrest.

The first piece of business at the convention was to devise a plan to support Chaplin. The group broke into committees to plan ways to raise the considerable amount of money needed for his bail. In addition, those in attendance passed a resolution; it read:

> We call on every man in the Free States, who shall go to the polls at the approaching elections, go with this motto

burning in his heart and burst from his lips: "CHAPLIN'S RELEASE, OR CIVIL REVOLUTION."

That revolutionary spirit continued throughout the convention. In fact, the Cazenovia Fugitive Slave Law Convention adopted one of the most radical attacks on slavery that had ever come out of an antislavery meeting. A letter written and endorsed by the convention members encouraged Southern slaves not to hesitate to violate the law in order to escape slavery, because their personal right to freedom superseded the property rights of their owners. The letter concluded: "by all the rules of war, you have the fullest liberty to plunder, burn, and kill, as you may have occasion to do so to promote your escape."

Emily and Mary were eager to do whatever they could to help raise bail for their good friend Chaplin, who was held in the Blue Jug, the jail they knew all too well from the days they spent there after their capture. It was unusual for a woman—even more so for a woman of color—to address a large audience, but Mary felt compelled to step forward at the convention and say a few heartfelt words about the important role that Chaplin had played in her life. Some in attendance described her effort as touching and eloquent.

JUMPING BAIL

On September 18, 1850, the same day that President Fillmore signed the Fugitive Slave Act into law, Chaplin appeared in court before Judge William Cranch. Chaplin sighed with relief when the judge set his bail at $6,000—a lot of money, no doubt, but Chaplin knew that his supporters would be ready and able to meet that bail.

But Chaplin wasn't freed. After he posted bail, he was handed over to the Maryland authorities, who took him directly to another jail, in Rockville. The charges against him in Maryland were far more serious than they were in the District of Columbia. In addition to two counts of larceny for attempting to steal slaves and two counts of assisting runaways to escape, he was charged

During the Cazenovia Convention, the organizers commissioned a daguerreotype, an early type of photograph, to send to William Chaplin in prison. Frederick Douglass is seated on the left side of the table. Mary Edmonson is the tall woman standing behind him with a plaid shawl. Emily Edmonson, also in plaid, is standing to the right of the abolitionist Gerrit Smith, the central figure.

with three counts of assault and battery with intent to kill for firing at the officers in the shootout. This time, the judge set Chaplin's bail at an exorbitant $19,000.

Chaplin languished in prison as those in the abolitionist community worked on raising the money for his second bail. Chaplin was not cut out for prison life. In the weeks that followed, his bruises faded and his wounds healed, but Chaplin was haunted by his memory of the beatings. Jittery and afraid, he questioned himself and his role in the abolitionist movement.

Emily and Mary joined other abolitionists who spent much of September 1850 making appearances in small towns across upstate New York raising money for Chaplin. The girls spoke and sang and begged and pleaded everywhere they could, every day they could, even on Sundays, which they didn't consider to be sinful because they believed that working to earn Chaplin's freedom was doing the Lord's work.

Three and a half months later, the entire $19,000 had been collected for Chaplin's second bail. In January 1851, Chaplin was released from the Montgomery County, Maryland, jail.

When he was released, Chaplin fled, refusing to return for trial and forfeiting $25,000 in bail money—the $6,000 that had been paid to the District of Columbia and the $19,000 paid to Montgomery County, Maryland. While they understood his anxiety about returning for trial and running the risk of going back to jail, Chaplin's supporters expected him to make an effort to raise funds to reimburse his donors. To their surprise and regret, Chaplin made very little effort to repay his debts. He refused to put himself at risk any longer. Chaplin retired and abandoned his antislavery work. It is unlikely that Emily and Mary ever saw their friend again.

≈ SIXTEEN ≈

Pardoned

ONTH AFTER MONTH, Drayton and Sayres remained in prison, waiting for their associates in the abolitionist movement to come up with a plan for their release. Drayton's patience ran out, however, when he learned that William Chaplin had been arrested and that money had been raised for his bail while Drayton and Sayres remained in the Blue Jug. How could his abolitionist associates have found so much money for Chaplin so quickly when he and Sayres had been sitting in jail for more than two and a half years?

Angry and annoyed, Drayton wrote to abolitionist William R. Smith and explained that Chaplin's supporters should not hold it against him if he revealed Chaplin's involvement in the *Pearl* escape. He wrote that the abolitionists "must not blame him if the chains weigh so heavily upon his limbs he should lose his power of endurance and seek that relief which his fellow citizens have not afforded him."

Not long after sending the letter, Drayton received word that his associates had renewed their efforts to get both of the captains pardoned and released from jail. With that understanding, Drayton agreed to maintain his silence, at least for a while.

The plan to free Drayton and Sayres required that the abolitionists convince a majority of the slaveholders to whom they owed fines to drop their claims for compensation. Drayton understood that his case was complicated by a Maryland law that required him to pay half his fines to the District of Columbia and half to the owners of the fugitive slaves. He also knew that his wife and his attorney, Daniel Radcliffe, had been going door-to-door making personal appeals and trying to persuade the slaveholders to waive their claim to the fine money. But months had passed and no visible progress had been made in his case, and at the end of the day, Drayton was still behind bars, still waiting.

While there were only 36 slave owners to visit, it took more than two months to execute the plan. Drayton learned that some of the slaveholders believed that Drayton and Sayres had served enough time for the crime and they signed the waiver with enthusiasm; others signed with some hesitation. Even years after the failed escape, a few still maintained that the captains should be hanged or, alternatively, tarred and feathered for their role in the escape.

A PRESIDENTIAL PARDON

Once a majority of slaveholders dismissed their claims against Drayton and Sayres, Senator Charles Sumner of Massachusetts wrote to President Millard Fillmore and asked him to pardon the captains. On August 12, 1852, President Fillmore signed a presidential pardon that released Drayton and Sayres from jail but left them financially responsible to the slave owners who did not waive their fines. While Drayton and Sayres were still required to pay thousands of dollars in fines, no one involved in the case expected that they would ever be able to do so.

As soon as the pardons had been executed, Senator Sumner arrived at the jail and demanded the immediate release of the captains. The U.S. marshal refused. He had received word from the Secretary of the Interior to hold the men until the next morning because the Virginia authorities wanted an opportunity to arrest and prosecute them for theft and the illegal transportation of two *Pearl* fugitives who had been owned by Virginians.

Stunned, Sumner hurried to the office of the *National Era* to consult with Lewis Clephane, the newspaper's 23-year-old business manager, who was in charge of removing the two men from the District of Columbia once they were released. Clephane shared Sumner's concern that like Chaplin, Drayton and Sayres would be released from the District of Columbia jail only to be immediately jailed in another jurisdiction.

When his Whig Party nominated Winfield Scott as their candidate in the coming election, President Millard Fillmore (1800–1874) knew his political career was over. With nothing at risk, he then pardoned captains Daniel Drayton and Edward Sayres. The pardon left the men financially responsible to those slaveholders who did not waive their fines.

Together, Sumner and Clephane returned to the jail to plead their case. Word of the presidential pardon had spread and local gossip included talk of a mob gathering at the jail. Sumner warned the marshal of the possibility of unrest if he waited any longer, so the officer grudgingly agreed to let the prisoners leave. As the door of the Blue Jug opened and Drayton and Sayres walked out of jail, the black prisoners inside cheered. After more than four years and four months of incarceration, Drayton and Sayres were free.

But that didn't necessarily mean that they were safe.

RACE TO FREEDOM

Clephane, a native Washingtonian, first ushered the captains to his home a few blocks away from the jail. Drayton and Sayres feasted on their first meal as free men while Clephane tried to line up a carriage and driver to take them to Baltimore later that night. Several days of heavy rain had damaged area bridges and washed out a number of roads, so many drivers refused to consider making the journey. Clephane eventually found a driver willing to make the treacherous trip, but for a substantially higher fee than normal.

By 10 p.m., Drayton, Sayres, and Clephane were on their way to the railroad station in Baltimore, where they hoped to board a train without being recognized. The unpaved roads were waterlogged and muddy. Near Bladensburg, Maryland, the river had overflowed its banks and the driver insisted they would have to turn back because the footing wasn't safe for the horses.

If they returned to Washington, they would be intercepted by the Virginia authorities and arrested. Unwilling to accept a change in plans, Clephane reached into his pocket and pulled out the large iron key that opened the door to the *National Era* offices. From the back seat, he reached forward and pressed the cold, hard metal into the back of the driver's head as if it were a gun and demanded that they keep going.

The driver urged his horse forward.

By the light of dawn, the carriage reached Baltimore. Drayton and Sayres were put on different trains: Sayres went directly to Philadelphia, while Drayton traveled to Harrisburg then east to Philadelphia. When he arrived in Philadelphia, Dr. Cleveland greeted Drayton and gave him $100 to help him get back on his feet, the same amount he gave Sayres.

Drayton took the cash, but no amount of money could make up for his compromised health. Drayton no longer resembled the able-bodied, 46-year-old man who first entered the Washington City Jail. He was withered and weak and unable to work; he walked stiffly and coughed often. He was unsure of his future, but grateful for his freedom.

SEVENTEEN

"The Last Two Drops of Blood in My Heart"

I N THE FALL of 1851, Emily and Mary Edmonson enrolled at New York Central College, in McGrawville, a small town in upstate New York. Emily was about 16 years old and Mary was about 18. They studied grammar, geography, and arithmetic, among other subjects, with the hope of someday founding a school for runaway slaves in Canada.

The girls made ends meet without Chaplin's financial support by working at school; the college paid female students three cents an hour for domestic work in the kitchen and dormitories and male students six cents an hour for agricultural work on the campus farm. They also received some support from abolitionist friends.

Their semester at school was interrupted by news that their younger siblings, Louisa and Josiah, were to be sold. As Emily and her siblings had feared at the time of their escape, their owner, Rebecca Culver, needed money. Her business agent had contacted Bruin to find out what the last two Edmonson children were worth. Valdenar, Culver's agent, then told Paul Edmonson that he would sell the children for $1,200 — either to the family or to Bruin.

At that time, Louisa, about 12 years old, still lived at home with her parents. Josiah, about 14 years old, had been hired out to live with and work for Valdenar, probably because his overseer considered the risk of Josiah's running away too great to send another one of the Edmonsons into the District of Columbia to be hired out.

Their father, now 65 years old, had gone north to try to raise the money, but he could collect only $100. Paul considered selling his 40-acre farm, but it was worth only $500. He owned farming equipment worth $35, and three horses, three cows, and five pigs, together worth $120. Just as was the case when he tried to raise money for Mary and Emily, if he sold everything he had, he would be left without the means to support himself and he would still fall far short of what he needed to buy their freedom.

Emily and Mary knew that it would be up to them to find a way to ransom their brother and sister. They feared that if they weren't able to raise the money, their siblings would have to endure the beatings and harsh conditions in the slave pens, as well as the threat of being sold south. They reached out to their abolitionist friends for help. This time, their mother, Milly, wanted to make an appeal to those who might be able to help the family. It is not known whether Milly had permission from her owner to travel out of the area. She would not have been considered a fugitive because her owner had faith that she would return; it was not conceivable that she would leave her family behind.

Their friends made arrangements for the girls and their mother to go to New York for a meeting with Harriet Beecher Stowe, author of the best-selling novel *Uncle Tom's Cabin*. At the time, Stowe was in Brooklyn visiting her younger brother, the same Rev. Beecher who had been instrumental in raising Emily and Mary's ransom. Stowe had learned about the Edmonsons from her brother, and she modeled several characters in her novel after Emily and Mary.

Harriet Beecher Stowe's Heartbreak

Harriet Beecher Stowe understood Milly Edmonson's sorrow. The year before she wrote *Uncle Tom's Cabin*, Stowe lost her son, Charley, to cholera. On December 16, 1852, Stowe wrote to friend and fellow abolitionist Eliza Cabot Follen:

> I have been the mother of seven children, the most beautiful and most loved of whom lies buried near my Cincinnati residence. It was at his dying bed and at his grave that I learned what a poor slave mother may feel when her child is torn away from her. In those depths of sorrow, which seemed to be immeasurable, it was my only prayer to God that such anguish might not be suffered in vain.

In addition to *Uncle Tom's Cabin*, Harriet Beecher Stowe (1811–1896) wrote more than 20 books, including several under the pen name Christopher Crowfield.

Stowe's grief inspired and motivated her to write her best-selling novel *Uncle Tom's Cabin*.

MEETING HARRIET BEECHER STOWE

Emily and Mary met their mother at Beecher's home in Brooklyn. The girls had not seen their mother in the four years since they moved north to attend college. They hugged and stared at one another; Emily noted that her mother was older, grayer, and more stooped than when she last saw her, but her spirit remained the same.

After all the necessary introductions, Milly settled in to tell Stowe about the pressure of raising children in the shadow of

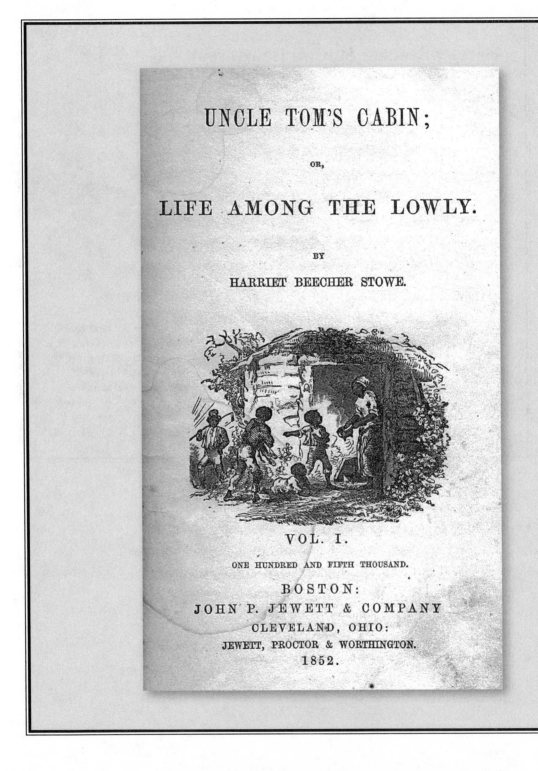

The Importance of *Uncle Tom's Cabin*

After Congress passed the Fugitive Slave Act, editor Gamaliel Bailey asked Harriet Beecher Stowe to write a serialized novel to be published in the abolitionist newspaper *National Era* in 1851. Stowe agreed and wrote *Uncle Tom's Cabin* in protest of the law and in sympathy with grieving slave mothers.

The novel appeared as a series of 40 weekly installments, or about one chapter each week. The first part of the series, titled "Uncle Tom's Cabin, or the Man That Was a Thing," appeared on June 2, 1851, filling most of the first page of the paper. (When it was released in book form, the title was changed to *Uncle Tom's Cabin; or, Life Among the Lowly*.) Stowe was paid $300 for 43 chapters, but she made her fortune in the later sale of the book that collected all the installments in a single volume.

Uncle Tom's Cabin became one of the most important books of the 19th century. It galvanized public sentiment against slavery, helping to ignite the Civil War. It became the best-selling novel of the 19th century and the second best-selling book behind only the Holy Bible in the number of copies sold that century. It remains influential today, with 150 editions in print worldwide.

Aspects of *Uncle Tom's Cabin* have been widely debated since its publication. Literary critics have condemned the work as sentimental and melodramatic. While many readers saw the character of Uncle Tom as strong, principled, and courageous, ultimately dying to protect other runaway slaves, others criticized him for using submissive behavior to get along with white society rather than standing up to his owner. In the decades after the book's release, the Uncle Tom character appeared in a number of other works that portrayed him as weak and subservient. The term "Uncle Tom" eventually became a negative label for a black person willing to use servility to win the approval of white people. *Uncle Tom's Cabin* nonetheless is credited with igniting a reform movement and mobilizing support for the abolitionist movement throughout the country.

In response to southern critics who asked Stowe to prove that the events in her novel were based in truth, in 1853 Stowe published a second book, *A Key to Uncle Tom's Cabin*. The book included "the original facts and documents upon which the story is founded, together with corroborative statements verifying the truth of the work." The book included a detailed account of the Edmonsons' story, based on the meeting she had in Brooklyn with Milly, Emily, and Mary.

slavery. She explained how she had taught her children to value liberty and to work for their freedom. She recounted the story of her daughter Henrietta, who had a chance to buy her freedom when she was sick and facing death. Henrietta's doctor told her not to bother buying her freedom because she would not live long. She told him: "If I had only two hours to live, I would pay down that money to die free." True to her word, Henrietta spent her savings and died a young—but free—woman. Milly couldn't have been more proud.

Stowe's 1853 book *A Key to Uncle Tom's Cabin* provides an account of Milly's comments. When Milly told Stowe about the horror she felt when six of her children were sold to a slave dealer after they attempted to escape on the *Pearl*, Emily and Mary chimed in with a bitter description of all slaveholders.

"Hush, children!" said Milly. "You must forgive your enemies."

"But they're so wicked," one of the girls responded.

"Ah, children, you must hate the *sin* but love the *sinner*."

"Mother," said one of the girls, probably Emily. "If I was taken again and made a slave of, I'd kill myself."

Milly stared at Mary and Emily in disbelief: How could her children have such unchristian things to say? Had slavery—and freedom—changed her daughters? "I trust not, child—that would be wicked."

"But Mother, I *should*. I know I never could bear it."

"Bear it, my child? It's they that bears the sorrow here is they that has the glories there," Milly said, referring to the promise of Heaven.

The discussion turned back to the family's common concern about ransoming Louisa and Josiah.

Emily could see that her mother's story touched Stowe profoundly. In their meeting, Milly explained to Stowe that her two

Mary and Emily, Emmeline and Cassy

The story of Mary and Emily Edmonson's attempted escape on the *Pearl* helped inspire Harriet Beecher Stowe when she was writing *Uncle Tom's Cabin*. In fact, Stowe based her characters Emmeline and Cassy in part on the stories of Mary and Emily Edmonson.

In *Uncle Tom's Cabin*, chapter 45, "Concluding Remarks," Stowe wrote:

The public and shameless sale of beautiful mulatto and quadroon girls has acquired notoriety from the incidents following the capture of the *Pearl*. . . . There were two girls named Edmundson [*sic*] in the same company. When about to be sent to the market, the older sister went to the shambles, to plead with the wretch who owned them, for the love of God, to spare his victims.

He bantered with her, telling what fine dresses and fine furniture they would have [if they became sex slaves for wealthy men in New Orleans].

"Yes," she said, "that may do very well in this life, but what will become of [us] in the next?"

They too were sent to New Orleans, but were afterwards redeemed, at an enormous ransom, and brought back. Is it not plain, from this, that the histories of Emmeline and Cassy may have many counterparts?

youngest children, Louisa and Josiah—"the last two drops of blood in [my] heart"—were to be sold away from her. She begged Stowe for her support in raising the money needed for their ransom.

Stowe pledged to help free Josiah and Louisa, promising Milly that she would help raise the money needed to free them and if it fell short, she would make up the difference. Milly thanked God—and Stowe—now that she was one step closer to having her family free.

True to her word, Stowe quickly raised the $1,200 needed to free Louisa and Josiah, but Valdenar, the agent for his sister-in-law, their owner, refused to honor their agreement. First, he increased his asking price by $300. When Stowe agreed to pay the higher price, he refused to sell them again, this time arguing that Josiah was still needed to work the fields. Stowe, unwilling to disappoint Milly, grudgingly agreed to accept the delay and continued the negotiations until the two youngest Edmonson children were safely at home with their mother.

Meeting Milly Edmonson

Harriet Beecher Stowe was impressed with Milly Edmonson from the first time they met. In *A Key to Uncle Tom's Cabin*, Stowe wrote:

> Milly Edmonson is an aged woman, now upwards of seventy. She has received the slave's inheritance of entire ignorance. She cannot read a letter of a book, nor write her own name; but the writer must say that she was never so impressed with any presentation of the Christian religion as that which was made to her in the language and appearance of this woman during the few interviews that she had with her. . . .

This is the only known photograph of Amelia ("Milly") Edmonson.

Milly is above the middle height, of a large, full figure. She dresses with the greatest attention to neatness. A plain Methodist cap shades her face and the plain white Methodist handkerchief is folded across the bosom. A well-preserved stuff gown and clean white apron with a white pocket-handkerchief pinned to her side, completes the inventory of the costume in which the writer usually saw her. She is a mulatto and must once have been a very handsome one. Her eyes and smile are still uncommonly beautiful but there are deep-wrought lines of patient sorrow and weary endurance on her face, which tell that this lovely and noble-hearted woman has been all her life a slave.

During their interview, Milly's story and her demeanor touched Stowe deeply. In Milly, Stowe had found a woman as humble and Christ-like as Uncle Tom, the protagonist in *Uncle Tom's Cabin*. She was impressed with Milly's character and her common sense. Stowe wrote to her husband, Calvin Stowe, that until she met Milly she had not met a "living example in which Christianity had reached its fullest development under the crushing wrongs of slavery." She continued: "I never knew before what I could feel till, with her sorrowful, patient eyes upon me, she told me her history and begged my aid."

EIGHTEEN

Emily, Alone

HARRIET BEECHER STOWE's friendship with the Edmonsons continued after Louisa and Josiah were freed. In the fall of 1852, Stowe made arrangements for Emily and Mary to attend Oberlin College in Ohio, one of the few schools in the country that accepted students without discrimination based on race or sex. In addition to the core subjects of mathematics, English, geography, and music, Stowe insisted that the girls learn basic housekeeping and sewing, which she argued would prove useful when they became teachers.

From the time they arrived on campus, Emily became concerned about Mary's health. Mary complained of "spinal difficulty," so at Stowe's recommendation, Emily applied hot and cold wet bandages to Mary's aching back as part of a water cure that was popular at the time. Mary remained thin and weak, plagued by a chronic cough, fever, and night sweats. The girls lived in the home of Henry Cowles, a minister and member of the Oberlin board of trustees, who provided Mary with healthy meals and plenty of rest. Nothing helped.

After several months, the sisters decided they wanted to go home to be with their family in Washington. Both of them longed to see their parents, and Emily worried that Mary's health was not improving and she might not survive to see her family again if they waited too long. Stowe discouraged them, arguing that travel to Washington in Mary's weakened state could make her worse. She may also have been worried that if their visit home was made public, the girls might be threatened by people who objected to their involvement in Stowe's latest book, *A Key to Uncle Tom's Cabin*, which documented the abuses of slavery. A full chapter of the controversial book discussed the Edmonsons. In any case, they did not make the trip.

By March of 1853, Mary's health had worsened further. Her symptoms were classic, but the news was still devastating when the doctor made a diagnosis: tuberculosis. By the end of April, the doctors warned that she would not live much longer. Emily hated to see her sister suffer, but she did not feel ready to let go. Emily had depended on Mary her entire life in slavery and in freedom as older sister, best friend, and spiritual guide. Emily's love for her sister defined who she was, and it shaped who she thought she would be in the future. Mary had been by her side through every experience in her life. What would she do without her?

Paul Edmonson came to Oberlin to be with his dying daughter; Milly couldn't make the trip. When he arrived on campus, Paul joined the 24-hour vigil at Mary's bedside. Helpless and heartbroken, Emily and her father dabbed sweat from Mary's forehead and wiped bloody spit from the corners of her mouth. They told her they loved her and listened to her struggle for each raspy breath in reply. They knew it wouldn't be long—no one could hang on to life like that for more than a few hours. Emily believed that someday she would see her sister again in Heaven, but still, it was impossibly hard to let go.

With her father and sister at her side, 20-year-old Mary Jane Edmonson died of tuberculosis on May 18, 1853. She was buried in Oberlin's Westwood Cemetery.

FROM STUDENT TO TEACHER

After the funeral, 18-year-old Emily wanted to return to Washington with her father rather than remain in Oberlin without Mary. Five years after attempting to escape on the *Pearl*, Emily was going home to the District of Columbia, but this time as a free and literate woman ready to build a life of her own.

Still, Emily felt incomplete without Mary. In the weeks after her return, she struggled to redefine herself as a young woman alone, rather than half of the duo known as the Edmonson sisters, Emily and Mary. On June 3, 1853, she wrote about her sister in a letter to Mr. and Mrs. Cowles, whose family she had lived with while at Oberlin:

> Though I am in Washington with all my dear friends, my heart still lingers around Oberlin, for I have left there beneath the green turf, one that I loved as I did myself, but we are far separated now, for she is in Glory and I am now in a land of chains and slavery. . . .

It took time to move beyond the sadness, but Emily wanted to follow through on the plans she and Mary had made to become teachers. Once again, Stowe provided Emily with the connections she needed to follow her dreams. Stowe recommended Emily to Myrtilla (Myrtle) Miner, the zealous headmistress at the Normal School for Colored Girls in Washington, D.C., a school dedicated to teaching black girls to become teachers themselves.

From their first meeting, Emily was struck by Miner's commitment. For a time Emily wondered whether she should instead return to Syracuse to stay with Jermain Loguen and his family, where she could work with the abolitionists. Stowe convinced her to become Miner's assistant, replacing a young Quaker woman who had spent a year at the school. Emily was to begin teaching primary school, with the understanding that she would move on to more advanced classes over time. A teacher! Emily would return to school, but this time as a teacher rather than a student. What would Mary think if she could see her now?

As they got to know each other, Emily listened to Miner tell stories about the founding of the school and its difficult beginnings. When Miner announced that she wanted to open a school for black girls in the nation's capital, many abolitionists and would-be supporters questioned her plan, telling her that they considered it futile and foolish. Even Frederick Douglass, an avowed proponent of education, discouraged her, considering the school an impractical and ludicrous idea because the community would never tolerate a school for black girls. Only Rev. Beecher of New York, the same man who had helped to raise Emily's ransom, thought that founding a school was an excellent idea; he promised to send money to buy furniture.

Myrtilla Miner (1815–1864) founded the Normal School for Colored Girls in order to train black students to become teachers.

Miner told Emily that she begged money from friends for the school. "Give me anything you have," she said. "Paper, books, weights, measures. I will make each one an object lesson for my girls." Ultimately, Miner returned to the District of Columbia with $100 and a teaching assistant. On December 3, 1851, the school opened with six students in a small apartment rented for $7 per month. Six months later, there were 41 students, and the classroom was equipped with carpet, desks, textbooks, and a small, select library donated by publishers and friends.

More than half of the students regularly paid the $1.50 monthly tuition.

Emily could see that Miner and her school had come a long way in a short time. The school recently had raised $4,300 to buy land and expand the facilities, and one of Emily's first tasks was to help Miner settle into the new campus, an abandoned three-acre farm in the District, which included a two-story main house and three small cabins, surrounded by shade trees, fruit trees, raspberry bushes, rhubarb plants, strawberry patches, and asparagus plants.

When Emily and Miner moved to the new location, there were no fences around the property or locks on the doors. In a letter to a friend, Miner wrote: "Emily and I live here alone, unprotected, except by God." Some in the community objected to the education of black girls. At times, troublemakers gathered near the school to insult the girls as they walked home after school. According to her 1851 memoir, Miner responded by yelling out the window: "Mob my school! You dare not! If you tear it down over my head, I shall get another house. There is no law to prevent my teaching these people and I shall teach them, even unto death!"

Vandals regularly stoned the house, trying to frighten Miner and Emily into leaving. Once, their house was set on fire; someone walking past woke them and helped extinguish the flames. At one point, the threats against the school had become severe enough that Miner had to seek help. She rushed into town and met with a night watchman. About 15 minutes later, four very burly men armed with clubs appeared on the school grounds and the troublemakers disappeared.

In order to defend herself and her school, Miner bought a revolver, and she and Emily learned how to shoot. When the troublemakers tried to harass them at the window of the schoolhouse with the weapon in plain view, she said she would shoot

The Normal School became Miner Teachers College in 1929 and the program is now part of the University of the District of Columbia. The college building, built in 1914, houses the School of Education at Howard University.

the first man who came to the door. "I have been seen practicing shooting with a pistol," Miner wrote in a letter to a friend, noting that, since that time "we have been left in most profound peace."

To further improve security, Miner invited Emily's parents to move into one of the cottages on the grounds, where Paul could cultivate a garden and Milly could work as a seamstress. When the Edmonsons moved onto the campus, bringing the family dog, their presence made Emily and the others at school feel safer, especially at night.

The school became an established and accepted part of the community. In the years that followed, Emily realized her dream of being a teacher—and because of her efforts, the next generation of Edmonson children did not have to struggle as much as she had to receive an education. Emily Brent, Emily Edmonson's niece, attended the Miner school and was a member of one of the first classes to graduate. After finishing her studies, Emily Brent moved to Wilmington, Delaware, where she began her career as a teacher, the second generation of Edmonsons to become educators.

Who Was Myrtilla Miner?

Myrtilla Miner, founder of the Normal School for Colored Girls, in Washington, D.C., had an interest in education her entire life. When Miner was a young girl, her father explained that he considered education beyond the basics to be superfluous, so he encouraged his daughter to drop out of school after a few years. She respected her father, but Miner couldn't bring herself to quit; she was curious and eager to learn.

Miner picked hops to earn money to buy books. She began to teach at age 15, and then wrote to the principal of the Young Ladies Domestic Seminary in Clinton, New York, asking for admission with the understanding that she would pay her tuition and room and board from her future earnings as a teacher. The principal accepted her terms.

Unfortunately, Miner's physical strength was not as great as her intellectual strength. As a first-year student, she suffered from severe spinal problems requiring back surgery. Her injuries kept her confined to bed, but she kept up with her studies, eventually attending class while lying on the floor at the back of the room.

After graduation, she accepted a teaching position in the Rochester, New York, public schools. She then moved to Providence, Rhode Island, followed by Whitesville, Mississippi, where she taught a plantation owner's daughter to read and write. In the South, she encountered slavery for the first time. The realities of holding men and women in bondage horrified her.

Miner thought that enslaved people should be educated. She asked the plantation owner—her employer—if she could teach the slaves on his plantation. He explained that it was a crime to teach a slave, suggesting she go north to teach the slaves if it was so important to her. That's just what she did.

One of the best descriptions of Miner on record comes from a letter Frederick Douglass wrote on May 4, 1883, to a trustee of the Miner school when asked to reflect about the life and mission of the school's founder. He wrote:

> It is now more than thirty years (but such have been the changes wrought that it seems a century) since Miss Miner called upon me at my printing-office at work, busily mailing my paper, the "North Star." . . . A slender, wiry, pale (not over-healthy), but singularly animated figure was before me, and startled me with the announcement that she was then on her way to the city of Washington to establish a school for the education of colored girls. I stopped mailing my paper at once, and gave attention to what was said. I was amazed, and looked to see if the lady was in earnest and meant what she said.
>
> I saw at a glance that the fire of a real enthusiasm lighted her eyes, and the true martyr spirit flamed in her soul. My feelings were those of mingled joy and sadness. Here, I thought, is another enterprise, wild, dangerous, desperate, and impracticable, destined only to bring failure and suffering. . . . To me, the proposition was reckless, almost to the point of madness. In my fancy, I saw this fragile little woman harassed by the law, insulted in the street, a victim of slaveholding malice, and, possibly, beaten down by the mob. . . .
>
> My argument made no impression upon the heroic spirit before me. Her resolution was taken, and was not to be shaken or changed. . . . I never pass by the Miner Normal School for Colored Girls in this city without a feeling of self-reproach that I could have [tried] to quench the zeal, shake the faith, and quail the courage of the noble woman by whom it was founded, and whose name it bears.

NINETEEN

Homecoming

ON APRIL 5, 1860, three generations of the Edmonson family gathered in the District of Columbia to celebrate the wedding of 25-year-old Emily. Her husband-to-be, 45-year-old Larkin Johnson, was a freed slave, widower, and father of four children: 17-year-old Benjamin, 16-year-old Mary, 13-year-old Martha, and 9-year-old Charles.

The celebration marked not only Emily's new status as wife, but also her new role of mother in a ready-made family. After the wedding, she planned to move to her new family's ten-acre farm in Montgomery County, Maryland, just a few miles away from where she grew up.

Larkin Johnson had lived in Montgomery County all of his life, so it is very likely that he had known the Edmonson family for years before marrying Emily. He had been freed in 1846 when his owner died. Little is known about Johnson's early life and his first marriage, except that his first wife, Lucy, died sometime in the 1850s.

In preparation for the wedding, Emily may have reflected on her past, as well as her future. She may have thought about her mother's frequent warning:

Now, girls, don't you never come to the sorrows that I have. Don't you never marry till you get your liberty. Don't you marry to be mothers to children that ain't your own.

On this day, both mother and daughter could think about how far they had come: Of Milly and Paul's children, Emily and her 13 brothers and sisters, all were known to have lived free, except one. Only John, the missing brother, may have remained enslaved at the time of the wedding. After the escape attempt on the *Pearl*, John was taken to New Orleans and sold from the showroom. There is no definitive evidence that he obtained his freedom, and there is no report that he ever saw his family in Washington again.

Emily and her family had overcome extraordinary odds. They had devoted their lives to the pursuit of freedom—both for themselves and for other family members—and their efforts paid off. Emily would never know her slave mother's sorrow: She would not have her babies sold away from her or be forced to raise ransom to buy them back. Emily was free, her husband was free, and every one of her children would be born free. Although they would face the challenges of racism and discrimination that dominated post–Civil War America, Emily and her family would spend every day of their lives in liberty, just as Milly Edmonson had dreamed.

Elizabeth Edmonson: Free to Marry

Some time in the 1840s, Elizabeth, the oldest of the Edmonson daughters, fell in love and wanted to marry John Brent. He was a "free dealer," meaning that his owner gave him permission to perform extra work for wages. His owner took the pay John earned as an employee for the War Department, but John kept the wages he earned working on weekends and evenings as a butler for wealthy Washingtonians. John saved his money and at the age of 25, he paid his owner $600 and bought his freedom.

Once he was free, John continued to work and save his wages, and a few years later he had saved $800 and purchased his father's freedom. He fell in love with Elizabeth—Lizzie—but, following her mother's advice, she refused to marry him until she was free. Brent sawed wood at night to make extra income and after two years, he had enough money to buy Lizzie's freedom and make her his wife.

Samuel's Story

The story of Samuel Edmonson's second escape from slavery was recorded by his nephew John Paynter and published in The Journal of Negro History *in 1916. The following is a summary of Paynter's account.*

Not long after Samuel Edmonson arrived in New Orleans, he was purchased to serve as a butler in the home of Horace Cammack, a prosperous cotton merchant. When he arrived at Cammack's home, Samuel immediately became infatuated with an 18-year-old slave named Delia Taylor, who served as a maid to Mrs. Cammack. They courted and eventually married; before long Delia gave birth to a son they named David.

Samuel and his family thrived until Cammack's son, Tom, returned from college. Tom disliked Samuel from the first time they met, and he did everything possible to make Samuel's life miserable. Eventually, the two clashed; Samuel wrote a letter explaining the situation and then he fled. It was not his intention to run away, but he did not feel safe with Tom. When he learned about the situation, Cammack ordered Samuel to return to the house and he sent his son out to live in the country. Samuel returned to the estate and to his family and willingly resumed his duties.

The following year, Cammack was killed in a violent storm while yachting with friends off the coast of Norway. Tom inherited Samuel and almost immediately decided to get rid of him. Rather than be sold to another family or risk becoming a field slave, Samuel decided to run away.

Samuel bought a set of forged free papers. Initially, he planned to escape up the Mississippi River, but he worried that that approach would be too dangerous. He went down to the riverfront to study the activity at the wharf and consider other options for escape. Lost in thought, he startled when a stevedore yelled at him to move out of the way. The sudden disruption broke his focus and gave him an idea: He could escape by impersonating a merchant from the West Indies in search of a missing bale of goods. Once he was in the islands, he would be protected by English law and free from slavery.

Samuel found a ship captain planning to leave that night for Jamaica. It wasn't a passenger ship, but the captain offered Samuel an extra bunk in the cabin, explaining that if he didn't mind roughing it, the seaman would be glad to have his company.

With only a few hours before his departure, Samuel hurried home to say good-bye to his wife and baby. Delia urged him to escape at once; Tom had already sent law enforcement officers out to look for him. Tearfully, Samuel left his wife and young son behind, aware that risking escape was the only way the family could possibly be reunited in the future. He slipped through the shadows and boarded the waiting ship.

Later that evening the customs officer boarded the ship to inspect the transit papers and found Samuel resting in the upper bunk of the ship's cabin. Had the officer been alerted to his escape? Was he looking for a runaway slave?

The captain spread the ship's papers out on a table in the cabin for inspection.

"Heigho, I see you have a passenger this trip," said the customs officer. "Samuel Edmonson, Jamaica, West Indies, thirty years old. General Merchant."

"Yes," said the captain. "Mr. Edmonson asked for passage at the last moment and as he was alone and we had a bunk not in service, I thought I'd take him along. He has a valuable bale of goods astray, probably at Jamaica, and is anxious to return and look it up."

"Well, I hope he may find it. Where is he? Let's have a look at him."

"Mr. Edmonson, will you come this way for a moment?" called the captain.

Samuel had been listening intently to the conversation. Now that he had to present himself, he murmured, "God help me," and jumped nimbly to the deck.

"This is my passenger," said the captain. To Samuel he said, "The customs officer simply wished to see you, Mr. Edmonson."

Samuel bowed and forced himself to stand at ease, resting one hand upon the table. He didn't look away or hold back when the customs officer looked him over, staring into his face, then reaching for his hands to assess their condition. Samuel let the inspector look at his hands, turning them over to examine his palms for signs of a lifetime of manual labor. Samuel's clean-cut appearance, callus-free hands, and trimmed fingernails weren't typical even of household slaves.

The customs officer shook Samuel's hand and said: "I hope you may recover your goods."

Samuel Edmonson thanked the officer and climbed back into his bunk. He had passed as a free man.

Samuel sailed on to Jamaica and then traveled without arousing suspicion on a schooner carrying a cargo hold full of wool to Liverpool, England. He took a job with an English merchant and saved his money. Although the details of their emancipation and reunion are unknown, three years after Samuel fled, his wife and young son were freed by Mrs. Cammack and joined him in England. The family then moved to Australia and supported themselves by raising sheep just outside Melbourne. Delia gave birth to three more children, but only two survived.

The details of their return were not documented, but sometime before 1868, the family returned to Washington, D.C. Samuel Edmonson died in 1907 at age 80.

Emancipation in the Nation's Capital

Enslaved people in Washington, D.C., were freed almost nine months before those in other parts of the country. On April 16, 1862—a date annually recognized in the District as Emancipation Day—President Abraham Lincoln signed a law that immediately freed all slaves living in the nation's capital. In addition, the bill allowed for slave owners to be compensated for their loss of property. Over a period of months, the Secretary of the Treasury paid nearly one million dollars to 966 slave owners to cover the liberation of 3,100 enslaved people.

Freedom was extended to millions of additional slaves in the South when President Lincoln signed the executive order known as the Emancipation Proclamation, on January 1, 1863. This act freed the three million slaves living in the ten Southern states that seceded during the Civil War. It also allowed freedmen, as the emancipated slaves were called, to enlist in the Union army.

But the Emancipation Proclamation did not ensure freedom for all. It did not apply to another one million enslaved people living in the five border states on the Union side, nor did it apply to Tennessee or certain areas of Louisiana and Virginia where Union forces were in control. It was not until the Thirteenth Amendment to the Constitution was adopted on December 16, 1865, that slavery was made illegal throughout the entire United States.

On April 16, 1862, President Abraham Lincoln signed the Compensated
Emancipation Act, which freed an estimated 3,000 slaves living in the
District of Columbia.

Death of a Martyr

Captain Daniel Drayton did not live long enough to see slavery outlawed. After his release from the Washington City Jail, he tried to raise money to live on by writing his memoirs. *Personal Memoir of Daniel Drayton*, written with help from Richard Hildreth, was published in 1854, two years after Drayton's pardon. It cost 38 cents for a hardcover copy and 25 cents for a paperback. The book sold only modestly.

Although the details of his life after prison are not well documented, it is known that Drayton never recovered his physical or emotional health. In the five years after his release from jail, Drayton moved restlessly from Philadelphia to Cape May, New Jersey; to Boston; to Staten Island; and finally to New Bedford, Massachusetts, a city with a large black community and a long history with the Underground Railroad.

On June 24, 1857, Drayton spent an evening with an old friend, a former slave who had attempted escape on the *Pearl* almost ten years before. Drayton, at that time a widower who had fallen out of touch with the rest of his family, told the man that he had come back to New Bedford to die in a place where he would get a proper funeral. Drayton's old friend didn't take him seriously.

A week later, Drayton checked into the Mansion House Hotel. He skipped dinner and told the front desk clerk that he did not wish to be disturbed. That evening he barricaded the door of his room and swallowed one and a half ounces of laudanum, a liquid form of morphine. Drayton then rolled up his pants legs, placed his feet in a pan of water, and sliced open the arteries in his ankles. When Drayton did not come out of his room the next day, the landlord broke down the door and found him dead.

Drayton had been correct: New Bedford did give him a celebrated farewell. Led by the mayor and the board of aldermen, the town honored the captain of the *Pearl* at a well-attended funeral at City Hall. More than half the mourners in attendance were from the New Bedford black community.

Drayton was buried at a cemetery in New Bedford, where a monument was erected to mark the grave of "Captain Drayton, Commander of the Schooner Pearl." His obituary in the local paper was titled "Death of a Martyr."

Time Line

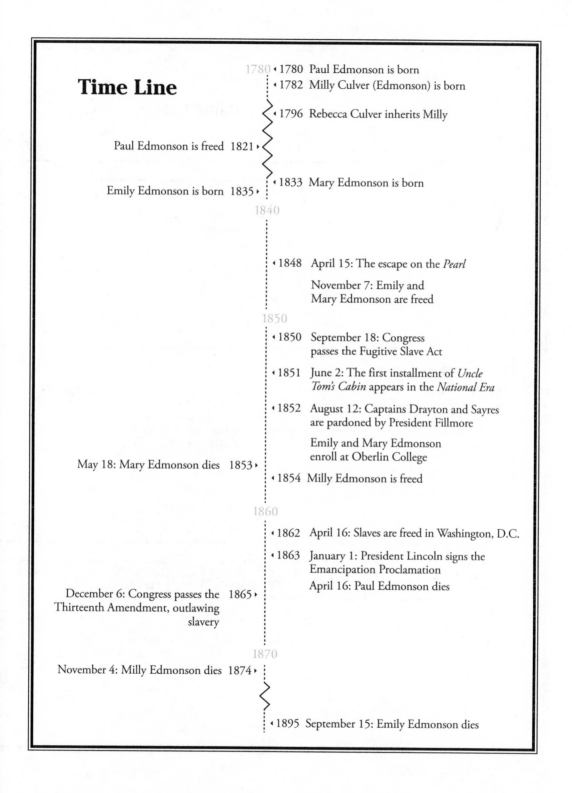

1780 ◂ 1780 Paul Edmonson is born

◂ 1782 Milly Culver (Edmonson) is born

◂ 1796 Rebecca Culver inherits Milly

Paul Edmonson is freed 1821 ▸

◂ 1833 Mary Edmonson is born

Emily Edmonson is born 1835 ▸

1840

◂ 1848 April 15: The escape on the *Pearl*

November 7: Emily and
Mary Edmonson are freed

1850

◂ 1850 September 18: Congress
passes the Fugitive Slave Act

◂ 1851 June 2: The first installment of *Uncle
Tom's Cabin* appears in the *National Era*

◂ 1852 August 12: Captains Drayton and Sayres
are pardoned by President Fillmore

Emily and Mary Edmonson
enroll at Oberlin College

May 18: Mary Edmonson dies 1853 ▸

◂ 1854 Milly Edmonson is freed

1860

◂ 1862 April 16: Slaves are freed in Washington, D.C.

◂ 1863 January 1: President Lincoln signs the
Emancipation Proclamation

April 16: Paul Edmonson dies

December 6: Congress passes the 1865 ▸
Thirteenth Amendment, outlawing
slavery

1870

November 4: Milly Edmonson dies 1874 ▸

◂ 1895 September 15: Emily Edmonson dies

The Edmonsons: A Family Tree

Paul Edmonson married **Amelia (Milly) Culver**
and they had 14 children:

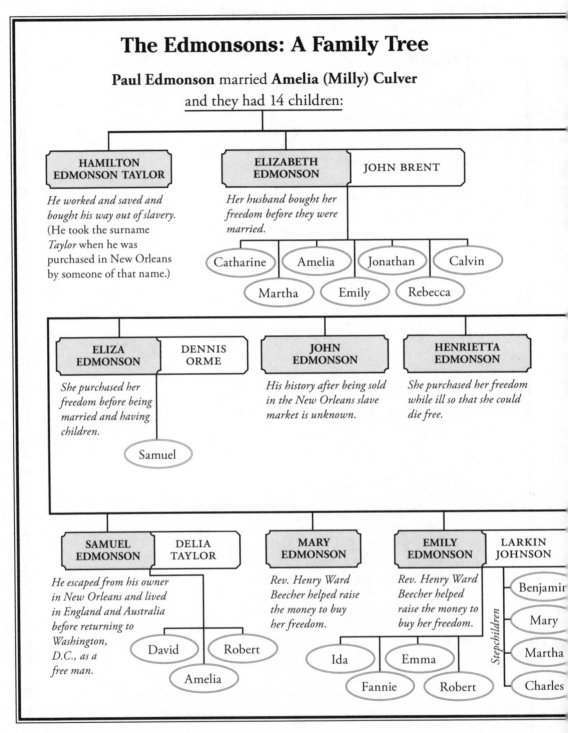

HAMILTON EDMONSON TAYLOR

He worked and saved and bought his way out of slavery. (He took the surname Taylor when he was purchased in New Orleans by someone of that name.)

ELIZABETH EDMONSON — **JOHN BRENT**

Her husband bought her freedom before they were married.

Catharine · Amelia · Jonathan · Calvin
Martha · Emily · Rebecca

ELIZA EDMONSON — **DENNIS ORME**

She purchased her freedom before being married and having children.

Samuel

JOHN EDMONSON

His history after being sold in the New Orleans slave market is unknown.

HENRIETTA EDMONSON

She purchased her freedom while ill so that she could die free.

SAMUEL EDMONSON — **DELIA TAYLOR**

He escaped from his owner in New Orleans and lived in England and Australia before returning to Washington, D.C., as a free man.

David · Robert
Amelia

MARY EDMONSON

Rev. Henry Ward Beecher helped raise the money to buy her freedom.

EMILY EDMONSON — **LARKIN JOHNSON**

Rev. Henry Ward Beecher helped raise the money to buy her freedom.

Ida · Emma
Fannie · Robert

Stepchildren
Benjamin · Mary · Martha · Charles

SOURCE: John H. Paynter, *Fugitives of the Pearl*, p. 204

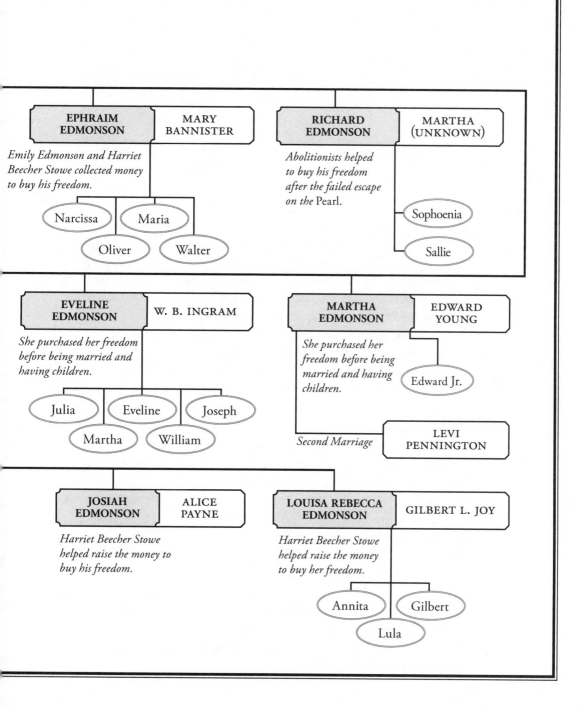

EPHRAIM EDMONSON — MARY BANNISTER

Emily Edmonson and Harriet Beecher Stowe collected money to buy his freedom.

- Narcissa
- Maria
- Oliver
- Walter

RICHARD EDMONSON — MARTHA (UNKNOWN)

Abolitionists helped to buy his freedom after the failed escape on the Pearl.

- Sophoenia
- Sallie

EVELINE EDMONSON — W. B. INGRAM

She purchased her freedom before being married and having children.

- Julia
- Eveline
- Joseph
- Martha
- William

MARTHA EDMONSON — EDWARD YOUNG

She purchased her freedom before being married and having children.

- Edward Jr.

Second Marriage — **LEVI PENNINGTON**

JOSIAH EDMONSON — ALICE PAYNE

Harriet Beecher Stowe helped raise the money to buy his freedom.

LOUISA REBECCA EDMONSON — GILBERT L. JOY

Harriet Beecher Stowe helped raise the money to buy her freedom.

- Annita
- Gilbert
- Lula

Sources and Notes

The following notes provide sources for quoted material. In some cases, the punctuation and spelling have been updated within quotations to reflect current usage, although the word choice remains unchanged.

Epigraph

"No man can tell the intense agony . . ." Frederick Douglass, *My Bondage and My Freedom*, ch. 19, "The Run-Away Plot." New York and Auburn: Miller, Orton & Mulligan, 1855, p. 284.

Chapter 1: A Mother's Sorrow

"I loved Paul very much . . ." Harriet Beecher Stowe, *A Key to Uncle Tom's Cabin: Presenting the Original Facts and Documents Upon Which the Story Is Founded Together with Corroborative Statements Verifying the Truth of the Work.* Boston: John P. Jewett & Co., 1853; replica: Elibron Classics; elibron.com, Adamant Media Corporation, p. 156.

"Well, Paul and me, we was married," Stowe, p. 156.

"I had mostly sewing . . ." Stowe, p. 156.

"I never seen a white man . . ." Stowe, p. 156.

"Now, girls, don't you never come . . ." Stowe, p. 157.

Chapter 2: Escape: April 15, 1848

"What will Mother think?" Stowe, p. 158.

"At that time, I had regarded . . ." Daniel Drayton, *Personal Memoir of Daniel Drayton, for Four Years and Four Months a Prisoner (for Charity's Sake) in Washington Jail.* Boston: B. Marsh, 1853 (e-book release December 8, 2003, Project Gutenberg; gutenberg.net; e-book #10401-8), p. 8.

"I no longer considered myself . . ." Drayton, p. 6.

Chapter 3: Against the Tide

"Be good children . . ." John H. Paynter, "The Fugitives of the Pearl," *The Journal of Negro History* 1, no. 3, July 1916. Reproduced by the Association for the Study of African American Life and History, Inc., Howard University, HU ArchivesNet, WorldCom (2000), huarchivesnet.howard.edu/0008huarnet /paynter1.htm> [May 22, 2010]; p. 2.

Chapter 5: Capture

"Do yourselves no harm . . ." Stowe, p. 159.

Chapter 6: Back to Washington

"Aren't you ashamed . . ." Paynter, "Fugitives," p. 6.

"Damn the law!" Drayton, p. 15.

"Lynch them!" Drayton, p. 15.

"This community is satisfied . . ." Drayton, p. 19.

"Let me say to you . . ." Drayton, p. 19.

"We advise you to be out of the way!" Drayton, p. 21.

"I cannot surrender my rights!" Drayton, p. 21.

"Down with the *Era*!" Drayton, p. 21.

"fearful acts of lawless and irresponsible violence." Keith Melder, *City of Magnificent Intentions: A History of Washington, District of Columbia.* Washington, D.C.: Intac, Inc., 2001, p. 126.

Chapter 7: Sold

"Have I not the same . . ." Stanley Harrold, *Subversives: Antislavery Community in Washington, D.C., 1828–1865.* Baton Rouge: Louisiana State University Press, 2003, p. 132.

"God bless you, sirs . . ." Harrold, p. 132.

"despised and avoided," Paynter, "Fugitives," end notes.

Chapter 8: Baltimore

"Last evening, as I was passing . . ." Drayton, p. 24.

Chapter 9: New Orleans

"Stop crying or I'll give you . . ." Stowe, p. 161.

"no room for the snuffles . . ." John H. Paynter, *The Fugitives of the Pearl.* Washington, D.C.: The Associated Publishers, 1930, p. 7.

Chapter 11: $2,250: The Price of Freedom

"Oh, my children . . ." Stowe, p. 163.

"Alexandria, Va., Sept. 5, 1848 . . ." Stowe, p. 163.

"I have often been utterly astonished . . ." Frederick Douglass, *Narrative of the Life of Frederick Douglass, An American Slave.* Boston: Anti-Slavery Office, 1845, ch. 2, p. 3.

Chapter 12: Ransomed

"When Henry is sent to me . . ." Lyman Abbott and S. B. Halliday, *Henry Ward Beecher: A Sketch of His Career with analyses of his power as a preacher lecturer, orator and journalist, and incidents and reminiscences of his life.* American Publishing Co., 1887; quinnipiac.edu/other/abl/etext/beecher/beechercomplete .html, p. 134.

"I had from childhood a thickness of speech . . ." Abbott, p. 135.

"The father! Do goods and chattel . . ." Abbott, p. 147.

"I thank you for that noise!" Abbott, p. 147.

"popping about like a box . . ." Abbott, p. 147.

"Take up another!" Abbott, p. 147.

"There, Mary, is that white man . . ." Stowe, p. 165.

"Received from W. L. Chaplin . . ." *Washington National Era*, November 30, 1848.

"You are free!" Stowe, p. 166.

"the sisters Mary Jane and Emily Catherine . . ." *National Anti-Slavery Standard*, November 30, 1848.

Chapter 13: The Trial of Captain Daniel Drayton

"It is said that some . . ." *Congressional Globe*, 30th Congress, 1st Session (December 1847–August 1849), p. 520.

"suffer death as a felon . . ." Drayton, p. 28.

Chapter 14: A Radical Education

"Slavery is a state of suppressed war . . ." *New York Independent*, December 21, 1848.

Chapter 15: Chaplin's Surrender

"We call on every man . . ." Hugh Humphreys, "Agitate! Agitate! Agitate! The Great Fugitive Slave Law Convention and Its Rare Daguerreotype" (monograph). *Madison County History Society Heritage*, no. 19. Oneida, N.Y.: Madison County Historical Society, 1994.

"by all the rules of war . . ." Humphreys.

Chapter 16: Pardoned

"must not blame him . . ." Mary Kay Ricks, *Escape on the Pearl: The Heroic Bid for Freedom on the Underground Railroad.* New York: HarperCollins, 2007, p. 228.

Chapter 17: "The Last Two Drops of Blood in My Heart"

"I have been the mother of seven children . . ." Henry Louis Gates Jr., *The Annotated Uncle Tom's Cabin by Harriet Beecher Stowe.* New York: W. W. Norton & Co., 2007, p. xxxv.

"If I had only two hours . . ." Stowe, p. 157.

"Hush, children!" Stowe, p. 167.

"The public and shameless sale . . ." Gates, p. 464.

"the last two drops of blood . . ." Stowe, p. 166; Paynter, *Fugitives*, p. 15.

"Milly Edmonson is an aged woman . . ." Stowe, p. 56.

"living example in which Christianity . . ." Ricks, p. 236.

Chapter 18: Emily, Alone

"Though I am in Washington . . ." Emily Edmonson to Mr. and Mrs. Cowles, June 3, 1853. Henry Cowles Papers, Box #3, Series: Correspondence, Personal; Folders: Aug.–Dec. 1852 and Jan.–July 1853; Record Group 30/27, Oberlin College Archives.

"Give me anything you have . . ." Ellen O'Connor, *Myrtilla Miner: A Memoir.* Boston and New York: Houghton, Mifflin & Co., 1851, p. 26.

"Emily and I live here alone . . ." O'Connor, p. 51.

"Mob my school! You dare not!" O'Connor, p. 56.

"I have been seen practicing . . ." O'Connor, p. 51.

"It is now more than thirty years . . ." O'Connor, pp. 21–25.

Chapter 19: Homecoming

"Don't you never marry . . ." Stowe, p. 157.

"Heigho, I see you have a passenger . . ." Paynter, *Fugitives*, p. 9.

"I hope you may recover . . ." Paynter, *Fugitives*, p. 9.

"Captain Drayton, Commander of the Schooner . . ." *New Bedford Evening Standard* (Massachusetts), July 2, 1857.

Bibliography

Abbott, Lyman, and S. B. Halliday. *Henry Ward Beecher: A Sketch of His Career with analyses of his power as a preacher lecturer, orator and journalist, and incidents and reminiscences of his life.* American Publishing Co., 1887 (www.quinnipiac.edu/other/abl/etext/beecher/beechercomplete.html).

Drayton, Daniel. *Personal Memoir of Daniel Drayton, for Four Years and Four Months a Prisoner (for Charity's Sake) in Washington Jail.* Boston: B. Marsh, 1853 (e-book release December 8, 2003, Project Gutenberg; www.gutenberg.net; e-book #10401-8).

Foner, Philip S., and Josephine F. Pacheco. *Three Who Dared: Prudence Crandall, Margaret Douglass, Myrtilla Miner, Champions of Antebellum Black Education.* Westpoint, Conn.: Greenwood Press, 1984.

Gates, Henry Louis Jr., and Hollis Robbins. *The Annotated Uncle Tom's Cabin by Harriet Beecher Stowe.* New York: W. W. Norton & Co., 2007.

Hanchett, Catherine M. "What Sort of People & Families . . . The Edmondson Sisters." *Afro-Americans in New York Life and History* 6, no. 2 (1982), pp. 21–37.

Harrold, Stanley. *Subversives: Antislavery Community in Washington, D.C., 1828–1865.* Baton Rouge: Louisiana State University Press, 2003.

———. "The Pearl Affair: The Washington Riot of 1848." *Records of the Columbia Historical Society, Washington, D.C.* 50 (1980), pp. 140–60.

Humphreys, Hugh. "Agitate! Agitate! Agitate! The Great Fugitive Slave Law Convention and Its Rare Daguerreotype" (monograph). *Madison County History Society Heritage,* no. 19. Oneida, N.Y.: Madison County Historical Society, 1994.

Loguen, Jermain Wesley. *The Rev. J. W. Loguen, as a slave and as a freeman: a narrative of real life.* Syracuse, N.Y.: J. G. K. Truair & Co., 1859; Sabin Americana, Print Editions, pp. 1500–1926.

Melder, Keith. *City of Magnificent Intentions: A History of Washington, District of Columbia.* Washington, D.C.: Intac, Inc., 2001.

O'Connor, Ellen. *Myrtilla Miner: A Memoir.* Boston and New York: Houghton, Mifflin & Co., 1851.

Pacheco, Josephine F. *The Pearl: A Failed Slave Escape on the Potomac.* Chapel Hill: University of North Carolina Press, 2005.

Paynter, John H. *The Fugitives of the Pearl.* Washington, D.C.: The Associated Publishers, 1930.

———. "The Fugitives of the Pearl." *The Journal of Negro History* 1, no. 3 (July 1916). Reproduced by the Association for the Study of African American Life and History, Inc., Howard University, HU ArchivesNet, WorldCom (2000), <huarchivesnet.howard.edu/0008huarnet/paynter1 .htm> [May 22, 2010]

Ricks, Mary Kay. *Escape on the Pearl: The Heroic Bid for Freedom on the Underground Railroad.* New York: HarperCollins, 2007.

Stowe, Harriet Beecher. *A Key to Uncle Tom's Cabin: Presenting the Original Facts and Documents Upon Which the Story Is Founded Together with Corroborative Statements Verifying the Truth of the Work.* Boston: John P. Jewett & Co., 1853; replica: Elibron Classics; elibron.com, Adamant Media Corporation.

Stowe, Harriet Beecher. *Uncle Tom's Cabin; or, Life Among the Lowly.* Boston: John P. Jewett & Co., 1852.

For More Information

About Harriet Beecher Stowe

Fritz, Jean. *Harriet Beecher Stowe and the Beecher Preachers*. New York: Puffin, 1998.

Hedrick, Joan. *Harriet Beecher Stowe: A Life*. New York: Oxford University Press, 1995.

Koester, Nancy. *Harriet Beecher Stowe: A Spiritual Life*. Grand Rapids, MI: Wm. B. Eerdmans Publishing Co., 2014.

Morretta, Alison. *Harriet Beecher Stowe and the Abolitionist Movement*. New York: Cavendish Square, 2014.

About Abolition and Slavery

Aronson, Marc. *Sugar Changed the World: A Story of Magic, Spice, Slavery, Freedom, and Science*. New York: Clarion, 2010.

Davis, David Brion. *Inhuman Bondage: The Rise and Fall of Slavery in the New World*. New York: Oxford University Press, 2008.

Horton, James Oliver. *Slavery and the Making of America*. New York: Oxford University Press, 2006.

Lowance, Mason, editor. *Against Slavery: An Abolitionist Reader*. New York: Penguin Classics, 2000.

Marrin, Albert. *A Volcano Beneath the Snow: John Brown's War Against Slavery*. New York: Knopf Books for Young Readers, 2014.

McNeese, Tim. *The Abolitionist Movement: Ending Slavery*. Reform Movements in American History. New York: Chelsea House, 2007.

Sanders, Nancy. *Frederick Douglass for Kids: His Life and Times*. Chicago: Chicago Review Preview, 2012.

Stewart, James Brewer. *Holy Warriors: The Abolitionists and American Slavery*. New York: Hill and Wang, 1997.

Thomas, William David. *William Lloyd Garrison: A Radical Voice Against Slavery*. Voices for Freedom. New York: Crabtree Publishing, 2009.

Slave Narratives and Oral Histories

Burton, Annie L. *Women's Slave Narratives*. New York: Dover, 2006.

Gates, Henry Louis, Jr. *The Classic Slave Narratives*. New York: Signet Classics, 2012.

Mellon, James. *Bullwhip Days: The Slaves Remember: An Oral History*. New York: Grove Press, 2002. First published 1988.

Perdue, Charles Jr. *Weevils in the Wheat: Interviews with Virginia Ex-Slaves*. Charlottesville, VA: University of Virginia Press, 1991.

Yetman, Norman. *Voices from Slavery: 100 Authentic Slave Narratives*. Mineola, NY: Dover, 1999.

———. *When I Was a Slave: Memoirs from the Slave Narrative Collection*. Mineola, NY: Dover, 2002.

In addition, many 19th and early 20th century slave narratives are in the public domain and are available to download free or for a nominal fee. Most are available in print editions as well.

Burton, Annie L. *Memories of Childhood's Slavery Days*, 1909.

Douglass, Frederick. *Narrative of the Life of Frederick Douglass*, 1845.

Du Bois, W.E.B. *The Souls of Black Folk*, 1903.

Hughes, Louis. *Thirty Years a Slave from Bondage to Freedom: The Institution of Slavery as Seen on the Plantation and in the Home of the Planter*, 1897.

Jacobs, Harriet. *Incidents in the Life of a Slave Girl Written by Herself*, 1861.

Northup, Solomon. *Twelve Years a Slave*, 1853.

Truth, Sojourner. *Narrative of Sojourner Truth*, 1850.

United States Work Projects Administration. *Slave Narratives: A Folk History of Slavery in the United States from Interviews with Former Slaves*, 1936–1938.

Washington, Booker T. *Up From Slavery: An Autobiography*, 1901.

Museums and Organizations of Interest

Alexandria Black History Museum
902 Wythe Street
Alexandria, VA 22314
(703) 746-4356
www.alexandriava.gov/BlackHistory

**Frederick Douglass National
Historic Site (National Park Service)**
1411 W Street, SE
Washington, DC 20020
(202) 426-5961
www.nps.gov/frdo

The Harriet Beecher Stowe Center
77 Forest Street
Hartford, CT 06105
(860) 522-9258
www.harrietbeecherstowecenter.org

**National Abolition Hall of Fame
and Museum**
5255 Pleasant Valley Road
Petersboro, NY 13035
(315) 366-8101
www.nationalabolitionhalloffameand
    museum.org

**National Underground Railroad
Freedom Center**
50 East Freedom Way
Cincinnati, OH 45202
(513) 333-7500
www.freedomcenter.org

The Pearl Coalition
(202) 650-5606
www.pearlcoalition.org

**Smithsonian National Museum
of African American History and
Culture**
1400 Constitution Avenue, NW
Washington, D.C. 20004
(202) 633-1000
www.nmaahc.si.edu

Acknowledgments

I offer special thanks to those who helped with this book, specifically:

Dr. Edna Green Medford, Professor of History at Howard University, for reviewing the manuscript;

the writing community at the Vermont College of Fine Arts, especially The Bat Poets and my VCFA critique group, for inspiring me as a writer;

Sarah Davies of the Greenhouse Literary Agency for representing my work;

Emily Parliman, Anne Winslow, Laura Williams, Steve Godwin, Brunson Hoole, Kelly Bowen, and the rest of the team at Algonquin;

Judit Bodnar for watching my p's and q's;

and, of course, Elise Howard, my editor. To paraphrase Wilbur in *Charlotte's Web*, it is not often that someone comes along who is a true friend and a good editor. Elise is both.

Index

Page numbers in italics refer to photos or illustrations and their captions.